FIRST IN
PEACE

Also by
Conor Cruise O'Brien

Parnell and His Party (1957)

Writers and Politics (1965)

To Katanga and Back: A UN Case History (1966)

Power and Consciousness (1969)

Shaping of Modern Ireland (1970)

States of Ireland (1974)

A Concise History of Ireland (1985)

The Siege: The Saga of Israel and Zionism (1986)

*Passion and Cunning: Essays on Nationalism,
Terrorism, and Revolution* (1988)

*The Great Melody: A Thematic Biography and Commented
Anthology of Edmund Burke* (1993)

*On the Eve of the Millennium: The Future of Democracy
Through an Age of Unreason* (1995)

*The Long Affair: Thomas Jefferson and the
French Revolution, 1785–1800* (1996)

Memoir: My Life and Themes (2000)

God Land: Reflections on Religion and Nationalism (2001)

FIRST IN
PEACE

HOW GEORGE WASHINGTON
SET THE COURSE FOR AMERICA

*An account of George Washington's
two presidential terms and of the dissensions that
accompanied the first term, were reflected in the
second, and echoed thereafter*

Conor Cruise O'Brien

WITH A FOREWORD BY CHRISTOPHER HITCHENS

DA CAPO PRESS
A Member of the Perseus Books Group

Designed by Pauline Brown
Set in 12.5-point Horley Old Style by The Perseus Books Group

Cataloging-in-Publication data for this book is available from the Library of Congress.

PUBLISHER'S NOTE
First in Peace incorporates substantial portions of Conor Cruise O'Brien's *The Long Affair* (1996), with the kind permission of the publisher of that earlier work. The author has written *First in Peace* with the aim of re-presenting that material and introducing new material so as to focus squarely now on Washington rather than Jefferson—on the art of subtle, magnanimous, and wide-resonating statecraft practiced by a president at a tender moment in America's history, especially in its relationship with the rest of the world.

First Da Capo Press edition 2009
ISBN-13: 978-0-306-81619-2

Published by Da Capo Press
A Member of the Perseus Books Group
www.dacapopress.com

Da Capo Press books are available at special discounts for bulk purchases in the U.S. by corporations, institutions, and other organizations. For more information, please contact the Special Markets Department at the Perseus Books Group, 2300 Chestnut Street, Suite 200, Philadelphia, PA 19103, or call (800) 810-4145, ext. 5000, or e-mail special.markets@perseusbooks.com.

10 9 8 7 6 5 4 3 2 1

Contents

Foreword

·

Cruiser
Christopher Hitchens

HOPING AS I AM to introduce both a book and a man, I here present to you Dr. Conor Cruise O'Brien, a man born in the year (indeed in the month) of the Russian Revolution and a man whose political and literary career has been devoted to the elucidation of French and American ones. Internationalist as Cruise O'Brien's career as a scholar and diplomat and politician has been, his Irishness has been no obstacle to him in the teasing out of the larger questions of our time. In this short volume, he crowns a long series of books and essays that have argued that the French Revolution, so far from being the continuation or extension of the American, was in fact a negation and not a consummation of the principles of 1776.

Cruise O'Brien is well aware that this conclusion conflicts with the most cherished hopes and dreams of a certain liberal or "Left" tradition, which some have even called "Jeffersonian." And it ought to be understood that his own re-evaluation of leftist and radical principles was neither an easy one in itself, nor conducted on a primrose path. There was a time when supporters of Irish independence, American independence, and French Jacobin ideals could all join to sing the same tune. Thomas Paine was one such and deserves honor for his efforts. But for Cruise O'Brien, such simplistic enthusiasm ignores the ever-present risk of tragedy and irony, not to mention the ever-threatening element of the will to power. Ever since his celebrated introduction to Edmund Burke's *Reflections on the Revolution in France*, published in 1968, he has been repeating (perhaps I should say updating) the admonitions of Burke against revolutionary zealotry.

Burke, in Cruise O'Brien's view, was indirectly pleading the Irish cause when he defended the American colonists and vilified the French regicides. Only by this close reading of the *Reflections* could we come to understand that Burke's stand on matters was not in fact as flatly conservative, let alone reactionary, as it seemed. Burke, so often thought of as an English royalist and Tory, was in fact an Irish Whig and quite possibly, in the time of penal laws imposed by Protestants, a "closet" Catholic. This furnishes us with a nice counterpoint in

Conor Cruise O'Brien, an Irish secularist with a socialist formation, who became among other things the editor-in-chief of a liberal London newspaper. But it was his service to Ireland that convinced him above all of the folly and wickedness of absolutist and righteous and messianic movements.

After the somewhat rare experience of a nonsectarian upbringing and education in strongly Catholic Ireland, Cruise O'Brien became a member of his country's diplomatic service. He served as minister in Paris from 1955 to 1956 and, after Ireland joined the United Nations in 1955 (which its wartime neutrality had prevented it from doing hitherto), as a member of the Irish delegation. In 1961 he was asked by Secretary-General Dag Hammarskjöld to act as his special envoy in the matter of Katanga's secession from the newly independent Congo. This led him into direct collision with the British and American governments, whose policy toward the issue he found to be cynical and duplicitous. For the remainder of the decade, Cruise O'Brien's name was closely associated with the anticolonial and "Third World" independence movements. He served as chancellor of the University of Ghana in the days of Kwame Nkrumah, and then as Albert Schweitzer Professor of Humanities at New York University. He also took a leading part in the cultural and intellectual battles of the Cold War, and he was one of those who first exposed the secret CIA funding of the prestige magazine *Encounter*. A volume of essays, *Writers and Politics*, published during this time, shows him firmly on the Left and wielding a pen that could strike real fear into an antagonist. (If I may be allowed a personal note, I remember picking up this book in a public library in Tavistock, Devon, in the summer of 1967 and forming the ambition to be able to write in that vein.)

Cruise O'Brien's return to his native Ireland, and his election as a Labour member of the Irish parliament in 1969, coincided with the reopening of the long-dormant crisis in the northern part of the country. A civil rights movement against the Protestant-dominated mini-state led to repression and state violence, which resulted in such a breakdown of order that British troops were deployed on the streets. And the Republican movement, which had long eschewed the use of physical force, underwent a split that led to the emergence of the so-called Provisional IRA and the use, once again, of the gun in Irish politics. This development was a hinge event in Cruise O'Brien evolution. Unlike many on the Left, he declined to identify the lethal romanticism of the IRA as a "liberation struggle," preferring to classify it as a green form of fascism. His commitment on this point led him

to join a coalition government, which took stern measures against the IRA and its sympathizers, and to write
a book (*States of Ireland*), which is generally agreed to be
the finest work, either literary or political, to have been
produced by the whole imbroglio.

His trajectory since then has taken him (in the view of
many, including myself) too far over to the Right and for
a time even as far as an actual embrace of Ulster Union-
ism. This is not the place to rehearse these disagreements:
rather it is the place to emphasize that Cruise O'Brien's
arguments have always been intelligible and internally
consistent. This is particularly true of his fidelity to Bur-
kean principles as these are applied to the contemplation
of (and opposition to) radical violence.

Most Americans are raised to think of their third
president, Thomas Jefferson, as a man of immense learn-
ing and dignity: a man of many parts who gave us the
noble words of the Declaration of Independence, the tran-
quil lawns of the University of Virginia, and the huge
benefits of the Louisiana Purchase. Recent years have
brought some distressing disclosures about his long affair with one of his slaves, Sally Hemings, and the chil-
dren that she bore him. Earlier hagiographic historians,
such as Dumas Malone, had downplayed or discounted
this possibility. But it was another "Long Affair" (as

Cruise O'Brien entitled his 1996 study of Jefferson and the French Revolution) that was to deal an even harder blow to his reputation.

On page 96 of this book there is an unexplained reference, the elucidation of which is necessary for a full understanding of Cruise O'Brien's critique of Jefferson. He writes that:

> Jefferson did not advocate entry into war, against monarchist England, on the side of the French Republic, although the mystical "Adam and Eve" side of him must surely have been attracted to the concept of a Franco-American alliance in the cause of Liberty.

This alludes to a celebrated letter of Thomas Jefferson's, written from Philadelphia to Paris on January 3, 1793. It was addressed to the American chargé d'affaires in Paris, William Short. Mr. Short, who had earlier been Jefferson's private secretary, had been sending home some dispatches that were very disobliging to the French revolutionaries, and that reflected Short's own sympathy with the defeated liberal faction that had centered around the Marquis de Lafayette. Jefferson replied in a tone of very severe reproof, defending the tactics of the Jacobins and excusing them for inflicting the occasional injustice in pursuit of a higher goal:

The liberty of the whole earth was depending on the issue of the contest, and was ever such a prize won with so
little innocent blood? My own affections have been
deeply wounded by some of the martyrs to this cause,
but rather than it should have failed, I would have seen
half the earth desolated. Were there but an Adam and an
Eve left in every country, and left free, it would be better
than as it now is.

For Cruise O'Brien, this letter possesses a dual significance. In its content, it shows a Jefferson who ap-
plauds the most ruthless methods and appears prepared
to countenance a "scorched earth" policy that would return humanity to a sort of "Year Zero." And in its timing, it reflects a Jefferson who, as secretary of state,
believes that he has George Washington on his side as a
sympathizer with France against England. A few days
before writing to Short, on December 27, 1792, to be
exact, Jefferson had been to see Washington. His own
recollection of the discussion was almost triumphalist.
Washington had expressed a desire for closer relations
with Paris and stated that "there was no nation on
whom we could rely at all times but France." Jefferson
expressed himself thus: "I was much pleased with the
tone of these observations. It was the very doctrine that
had been my polar star, and I did not need the successes

of the Republican arms in France lately announced to us, to bring me to these sentiments." (The reference here was to the Battle of Valmy in September 1792, which had opened a series of French military victories against European monarchist intervention.) Jefferson was both writing and thinking as if history was on his side, and George Washington too. Cruise O'Brien's purpose is to demonstrate that he was radically wrong on both counts.

The keyword in this narrative is *hubris*. Not just the hubris of Jefferson himself, who had to ignore or overlook a mountain of conflicting evidence in order to come to those conclusions about either his French Revolution or his president, but the hubris of the French revolutionaries themselves. In the year that followed Jefferson's incautious and revealing letter to Short, he was to suffer a whole series of political reverses, most of them inflicted on him by his friends rather than his enemies.

The great mistake of the French was to imagine that they could treat George Washington as a mere figurehead and appeal to American public opinion over his head, as it were. The associated mistakes of Thomas Jefferson were, first, to think that he could privately collude with this French demagogic populism and, second, to persuade himself that George Washington would never get to hear about his double dealing. These illusions were perhaps excusable. At that time, bonfires and parades and public dinners and celebrations were commonplace all across the United States, hailing the emergence of another revolutionary republic that would end American isolation and returning the solidarity with France that had marked the American war of independence. Those of Republican bent were busily setting up "Democratic" societies and clubs, which unofficially constituted the political base of Thomas Jefferson. As secretary of state, however, he had to preserve the dignified appearance of one who was above the fray.

This pose was made impossible by his French allies, who fatally overstepped. They sent a new envoy to the United States, Edmond-Charles Genêt by name, who landed in Charleston in May of 1793. The date was inauspicious: George Washington had just disappointed Jefferson by issuing a "Proclamation" declaring the United States to be "impartial" in the quarrel between France and Britain. (He had also disappointed his treasury secretary, Alexander Hamilton, by failing to use the stronger word "neutral.") Genêt made his way from Charleston to Philadelphia, not waiting to present his diplomatic credentials to President Washington before embarking upon a barnstorming campaign to rouse American support for the French side. To say that he overplayed his hand is to say the least of it. As Cruise O'Brien demonstrates, he was in receipt of instructions from

Paris that amounted to a gross interference in American internal affairs. The Executive Council told him that he was to induce the Americans to side with France, and that if they demurred he was to remind them that the demands were "no more than the just price of the independence which the French nation won for them" (page 90). It might be true that French arms had greatly aided the cause of American independence but—as George Washington icily underlined to Genêt, by retaining the portraits of King Louis and Marie Antoinette on his walls—that had been under a previous regime.

Americans might well wear revolutionary cockades in solidarity with French aspirations, but under no circumstances were they going to let their president's dignity or authority be impugned or undermined by a loquacious Frenchman. And this brings me to another Cruise O'Brien reference that requires a little elucidation. On page 105 we read that "Genêt was shaken, but by no means chastened, by the repercussions of his defiance of the government." This alludes to Genêt's extraordinary rashness, while acting under diplomatic cover, in continuing to commission French privateers from American ports, to harass English shipping. In July 1793, having already annoyed Washington by his public flamboyances, he insisted that a British vessel captured by the

French be renamed (as *La Petite Démocrate*), refitted, and relaunched as a privateer. Nor did he wait for an American answer to his demand. The ship actually set sail while the Cabinet was still discussing the matter. Washington's fury at this insolence was matched only by that of Alexander Hamilton, who wanted the vessel fired upon before it could leave its moorings. It was decided to ask the French government to recall Citizen Genêt to Paris, and Thomas Jefferson drew the unpleasant job of composing the letter that made the request.

As if to underscore the moral victory that he had won, Washington went on to extend the hand of magnanimity to Genêt, who was quick to realize the probable fate that awaited him on his return. He petitioned to remain in America, the country whose politics he had been trying so brazenly to subvert, and the president granted him his request. (He was to marry the daughter of Governor George Clinton of New York, and to settle down as a peaceful farmer.) From that point onward, it is safe to say, the partisans of French Jacobinism in the United States were in political eclipse, and there was never again the possibility that America would be drawn into the Napoleonic wars on the French side. Indeed, it was to be French losses and reverses, in Haiti and elsewhere, that would ironically provide Jefferson

as president with the historical opportunity of the Louisiana Purchase.

This, however, was well in the future. For the moment, Jefferson's career was over. He managed to wrap
up the Genêt affair and its ramifications with as much
dignity as he could muster, and then left office to return
to his Monticello estate. For the remainder of George
Washington's tenure of the presidency, it was the political faction associated with Alexander Hamilton and the
Federalists that was to predominate. This dominance
showed itself with great clarity in the events known
to history as the "Whiskey Rebellion." Essentially a
protest against federal taxation, in this case on liquor,
and essentially confined to western Pennsylvania, this
provincial revolt in late 1794 took on more lurid political
colors because of the revolutionary rhetoric exported
from France. At one point, the leadership of the rebellion
even thought of grandly entitling itself a "Committee
of Public Safety" on the Jacobin model. And the occasion provided an opportunity for the newly formed
"Democratic-Republican" societies to engage in agitation. The term used by Washington for these political
clubs was "self-created societies": a tautology in a way
but an expression of his contempt for their populist
claims. As Cruise O'Brien cleverly points out, this an-

tagonism on his part was by no means new. As long ago as 1786 he had objected to a "Patriotic Society," formed to instruct the delegates from an area of Virginia, in the following terms:

> To me it appears much wiser and more politic to choose able and honest representatives and leave them in all national questions to determine from the evidence of reason and the facts which shall be adduced, when internal and external evidence is given to them in a collective state. What certainty is there that societies in a corner or remote part of a state can possess a knowledge which is necessary for them to decide? What figure then must a delegate make who comes [to the capital] with his hands tied and his judgment forestalled? His very instructors perhaps (if they had nothing sinister in view), were they present at all the information and arguments which would come forward might be the first to change sentiments?

Cruise O'Brien does not say so explicitly, but these words make an excellent "fit" with the principles adumbrated by Edmund Burke in his celebrated address to the electors of his Bristol constituency, advising them as their member of parliament that he would not be their

delegate but rather their representative, and that he could
not agree to be bound by their instructions. He does,
however, make the comparison between Washington and
Burke in pointing out that both had foreseen the likeli-
hood of the French Revolution mutating into a military
dictatorship.

At almost the same time as the Whiskey Rebellion
came the news of a treaty with Great Britain, which became known—after the chief justice who negotiated it—
as the Jay Treaty. Widely regarded by populists and
Democrats as a sellout, its terms ignited a huge series of
public demonstrations and a tremendous press campaign
against Washington himself. In his correspondence, and
in the contacts he maintained with those still active in
politics, Jefferson helped fuel the support for the Pennsylvania rebels and the opposition to the treaty. It was
a very difficult time for George Washington, but with a
combination of military resolve and political skill, he
swiftly put down the whiskey rebels and outpointed the
congressional opposition to the agreement with London
negotiated by Jay. His key ally in both these victories
was Alexander Hamilton, and it was to Hamilton that
Washington turned when it came time, in the fall of
1796, for him to consummate his victory by publishing
his "Farewell Address." Perhaps never before in history
had a man of such political power agreed to surrender it:

certainly nobody has ever provided a better illustration
of the maxim that one does best to quit when one is
ahead. By the conclusion of his second term, George
Washington had helped set the course that the United
States was to continue to follow. Domestically, he had
decided in favor of the Hamiltonian system of commerce
and industry, symbolized by the setting up of a central
bank. Internationally, he had positioned the country between the warring powers of France, Spain, and Britain in
such a way as that it might profit from the rivalry without being directly drawn into it. This had meant a defeat
for the southern and agrarian forces, and for the pro-
French revolutionary romantics, both factions being
(perhaps oddly) led by the same man. Thomas Jefferson's political brilliance was of course not to be perma-
nently frustrated, but by the time he acceded to the
presidency himself it was on terms and conditions that
Washington, Hamilton, and Adams had helped to frame
and install.

Washington's achievement was so large, and his execution of it so impeccably and magnanimously timed,
that the attacks on him, even by men of the stature of
Thomas Paine, appear in retrospect to be petty and irrel-
evant. It is not really necessary for Cruise O'Brien to
speculate that Paine's polemic was written by a paid hack
working for the French: the stuff was poor and it missed

its mark by a mile and this is all that needs to be said. He is closer to his true form when he offers a generous defense of Jefferson's own Janus-faced conduct in this decisive era: a touch of magnanimity in itself. This book greatly assists us in elucidating the statecraft of America's first president.

Part One

WASHINGTON'S
FIRST TERM

I

ON THE FOURTEENTH DECEMBER, 1799, after a brief illness [Washington] departed this life at Mount Vernon, aged sixty-eight years. On receiving this mournful intelligence, Congress, then in session at Philadelphia passed the following resolution:

Resolved that the speaker's chair should be shrouded in black, that the members should wear black during the session, and that a joint committee from the Senate and the House, be appointed to devise the most suitable manner of paying honour to the Man, *first in war, first in peace and first in the hearts of his countrymen* [emphasis mine].

The author of the funeral oration on the death of George Washington was Major-General Henry Lee, a member of Congress from Virginia. In its context the most relevant phrase ran as follows:

First in war, first in peace and first in the hearts of his countrymen, he was second to none in the humble and enduring scenes of private life. Pious, just, humane, temperate and sincere; uniform, dignified and commanding; his example was as edifying to all around him as were the effects of that example lasting.[1]

During the revolutionary war, Henry Lee had been an exceptionally brilliant cavalry commander who came to be known as "Light-horse Harry."

When Washington first became president, Henry Lee initially shared the reservations of many Virginians about him, seeing him rightly as a person who did not see himself as a Virginian first, and only secondarily an American. But as soon as Washington's presidency began to take shape, Henry Lee rallied completely to his support, and was soon briefing him on Jefferson's attempts to subvert Washington in Virginia.

II

GEORGE WASHINGTON WAS INAUGURATED as president of the United States on April 30, 1789. In August of the same year the first reports of the French Revolution began to reach America. On October 13, 1789, Washington wrote as follows to his close wartime friend and confidant Gouverneur Morris, who was at that time in France, a wealthy private citizen on business at the start of a nine-year residence in Europe during which Washington was to appoint him to represent the United States from 1792 to 1794 as minister plenipotentiary in France:

> The revolution which has been effected in France is of so wonderful a nature that the mind can hardly realize the . fact. If it ends as our last accounts to the first of August predict; that nation will be the most powerful and happy in Europe, but I fear that though it has gone triumphantly through the first paroxysm, it is not the last it has to

encounter before matters are finally settled. In a word, the revolution is of too great magnitude to be effected in so short a space and with the loss of so little blood. The mortification of the King, the intrigues of the Queen, and the discontent of the Princes and the Noblesse will foment divisions, if possible, in the national assembly and will avail themselves of every *faux pas* in the formulation of the constitution if they do not give a more open active opposition. To these, the licentiousness of the People on one hand and sanguinary punishment on the other will alarm the best disposed friends to the measure and contribute not a little to the overthrow of their object. Great temperance, firmness and foresight are necessary in the movements of that Body. To forbear running from one extreme to another is no easy matter, and should this be the case, rocks and shoals not visible at present may rack the vessel.[2]

This is a very remarkable passage for three reasons. First, it is a sober and bleak analysis of the probable future progress of the revolution, closely comparable, though even more pessimistic, to that propagated in Britain a little earlier (August 9, 1789) by Edmund Burke.[3] Second, Washington's letter to Gouverneur Morris has no resemblance to the uniformly respectful *public* statements of the American president about the French

Revolution during its first few years. Washington knew that the American public was enthusiastic about the French Revolution during that time, and he had no intention of unnecessarily or prematurely risking a confrontation that might endanger his popularity and influence, immense though these remained. Third—and most important—the assessment offered confirmation that the president was preparing for a radical change in American foreign policy.

It was a *confirmation* rather than a notification: a confirmation of a desired policy shift already signaled. On October 3, 1789, Washington had asked Morris in his capacity as an American citizen resident abroad by choice "to take soundings whether the British incline to a treaty of commerce with the United States, and if so, on what terms."[4]

Taken together, those two letters to Morris amount, in substance if not in form, to a projected reversal of alliances. Washington clearly understood that the proposed treaty of commerce between the United States and Great Britain would infuriate the French, and also infuriate the warmest enthusiasts for the French Revolution in America, especially in the Southern states. All the same, this is what Washington was now aiming at, and he was to achieve his aim, eventually, although it took him probably somewhat longer than he had at first hoped.

On January 21, 1790, Washington invited Thomas Jefferson to become his secretary of state. Jefferson does not appear to have been informed about Washington's misgivings about the future of the French Revolution, misgivings the president had never made public. Much more important, Jefferson was certainly not informed about the opening of negotiations, through Morris, with the British government for an Anglo-American treaty.

This was a startling omission since, within the American Cabinet, the negotiation of treaties was primarily a matter for the secretary of state, though actual decisions on all important matters always rested with the president himself. Yet the secretary of state was to learn that his president had authorized negotiations with the British for a treaty only through an accidental disclosure by a third party at the end of March 1791, when the negotiations had been in (rather shaky) progress since October 1789. This meant that Jefferson had been kept in ignorance of the treaty negotiations for more than a year after he took office in February 1790.

The close relationship between Washington and Gouverneur Morris went back a long way. As the *Dictionary of American Biography* records:

On an official visit of inspection [on behalf of New York State] to the army at Valley Forge, early in 1778, Morris came into close contact with Washington to whom he remained devoted for life, and of whose military policies he became perhaps the most important and able defender in Congress. Elected to the Pennsylvanian Delegation at the Constitutional Convention of 1787 he took more part in the debates of that body than any other member on the floor, not even excepting James Madison. He loyally accepted the bundle of compromises which made up the Constitution and used his incomparable skill in putting the document into its final literary form.[5]

Gouverneur Morris went to Europe early in 1789, did much business there, and early in 1792 was appointed by Washington—against Jefferson's advice—as minister plenipotentiary to France.

J. A. Carroll, in his 1961 study, "George Washington,"[6] says: "While Hamilton served as secretary of the treasury and Jefferson as secretary of state, Washington solicited advice from them almost equally." The actual records of Washington's first presidential term, in which both Jefferson and Hamilton served as Cabinet officers, tell us something quite startlingly different.

Most American historians, following Dumas Malone, and (in part) Julian P. Boyd, suggest that Washington only slowly lost confidence in Jefferson as his secretary of state. To me, the record suggests something else: that Washington never had confidence in Jefferson as his secretary of state in what concerned relations with by far the two most important aspects of American foreign relations: relations with Great Britain and with France. If he had had confidence in Jefferson in those areas he would have informed him of his misgivings about the French Revolution and about the negotiations he had opened with Britain through his trusted friend Gouverneur Morris. He is not known to have informed Jefferson about the misgivings on Jefferson's taking office. He certainly didn't inform Jefferson about the second and more important transaction.

The member of the Cabinet in whom he placed his confidence in relation to America's most important foreign affairs—relations with Great Britain and France—was not his secretary of state but his secretary of the treasury, Alexander Hamilton, as I propose to show.

III

At the end of March 1791 William Carmichael, American chargé d'affaires at Madrid, informed the secretary of state that he had seen in Madrid extracts from the president's letter to Gouverneur Morris (dated October 13, 1789) authorizing him to enter into a private negotiation for certain objects with the British Cabinet. He supposed these extracts to have been sent secretly by the British minister to the British ambassador at the court of Spain, for the purpose of inciting a jealousy on the part of Spain in regard to the movements of the United States, and thus to have an influence on a discussion then pending between England and Spain. Mr. Carmichael supposed the extracts were mutilated or forged. Mr. Jefferson recommended that a genuine copy of the letter should be sent to him, with permission to use it as he should think proper.[7]

So it was that in early April 1791, Thomas Jefferson learned for the first time of the opening of negotiations by Washington with Britain through Gouverneur Morris a year and five months earlier. Apparently the British, for the benefit of their relations with Spain, had leaked word of their negotiations with the Americans.

Washington was clearly deeply embarrassed by Jefferson's discovery of his letter to Morris, and his reply to Jefferson reflects his embarrassment:

To Thomas Jefferson, Secretary of State; Richmond, 13 April, 1791.

Your letter of the 2nd. Came to my hands at this place. Part of it did, as you supposed, and might well suppose, astonish me exceedingly. I think it not only right, that Mr. Carmichael should be furnished with a copy of the genuine letter to Mr. Morris, but think that Mr. Morris should know the result of his conferences with the Duke of Leeds at the court of Madrid. The contents of my public letters to him you are acquainted with. My private ones were few *and there was nothing in any of them, respecting England or Spain* [emphasis mine]. How it comes to pass, therefore, that such interpretations, as the extracts recite, should be given he [who] best can account for.

This is a confused and confusing letter, reflecting the embarrassment of the writer. To say that "there was nothing in any of [his private letters] respecting England or Spain" seems simply to be untrue: the letter to Gouverneur Morris, opening an unofficial negotiation with Britain, was unquestionably intended to be private, except from the British, and had remained so until it was leaked. But Washington knew it no longer remained so because he had been forced to send a copy of it to Jefferson. So the denial appears to be not merely false but futile: interesting only as evidence of an embarrassment such as the resourceful Washington very seldom experienced. Indeed this letter seems to be unique in all his correspondence.

Jefferson was naturally furious at this clear evidence that he, as secretary of state, had not enjoyed the confidence of his president ever since he entered the office. His language on receiving Washington's letter suggested that he was contemplating resignation. He seems, however, to have set too much store by his position as secretary of state, even without his president's confidence, to lay down the position. To remain a member of Washington's Cabinet, privy to all its transactions, while secretly undermining it, was an advantageous position, and one well suited to Jefferson's devious temperament.

We now know that it was Washington's secretary for the treasury, Alexander Hamilton, and not his secretary of state for foreign affairs, Thomas Jefferson, who enjoyed Washington's confidence, not only in relation to the treasury, but also in connection with by far the most important aspects of American foreign relations: relations with Great Britain and with revolutionary France.

Hamilton's pivotal position in American policymaking is well set out in the fullest modern biography of Hamilton by far: that of Ron Chernow.[8]

Chernow writes:

[Hamilton] was the messenger from a future that we now inhabit. We have left behind the rosy agrarian rhetoric and slaveholding reality of Jeffersonian democracy and reside in the bustling world of trade, industry, stock markets, and banks that Hamilton envisioned. (Hamilton's staunch abolitionism formed an integral part of his economic vision.) He has also emerged as the uncontested visionary in anticipating the shape and powers of the federal government. At a time when Jefferson and Madison celebrated legislative power as the purest expression of the popular will, Hamilton argued for a dynamic executive branch and an independent judiciary, along with a professional military, a central bank and an advanced financial system. Today, we are indisputably the heirs to Hamilton's America, and to repudiate his legacy is, in many ways, to repudiate the modern world.

Despite clear evidence of Washington's silent lack of confidence, the first *public* indication that it was Hamilton rather than Jefferson who enjoyed the president's confidence in major aspects of foreign affairs came in the period from the spring of 1790 to the spring of 1791. Benjamin Franklin died early in the spring of 1790, and news of his death reached New York on April 22, 1790. On the same day, James Madison, Jefferson's friend and ally, moved in the House of Representatives that the members should wear badges of mourning for a month. The House agreed, apparently without a debate. The Senate, always more responsive to Washington's (and Hamilton's) influence than the House, did not mourn: a proposal to mourn was moved in the Senate, but had to be withdrawn for want of a seconder. As Jefferson succinctly reported to William Short in Paris: "The House of Representatives resolved to wear mourning, and does it. The Senate neither resolved it nor do it."

Jefferson also, as he later recalled, suggested to Washington, but in vain, that the executive should follow the example of the House: "I proposed to General Washington that the Executive Department should follow the example of the House and not of the Senate in this matter.

I proposed to General Washington that the Executive department should wear mourning. He declined it, because he said he did not know where to draw the line, if he once began that ceremony."

As was so often the case, Washington was being less than candid with his secretary of state. This was *not* a matter of not knowing where to draw the line. Washington knew very well where to draw the line, and he was drawing it against the friends of revolutionary France in America, the most influential of whom was his secretary of state, Thomas Jefferson.

At this stage, it does not appear that the topic of the French Revolution had yet been overtly introduced into the American discussion of how, or whether, to honor the memory of Benjamin Franklin. But, as subsequent events were to make amply clear, it was conflicting feelings about the French Revolution that shaped the whole Franklin episode. Franklin, representative of the United States in France throughout the American Revolution, had become the symbolic figure, for both the French and Americans, of Franco-American friendship. And by 1790, Franco-American friendship had come to mean specifically *friendship with the French Revolution*. Jefferson and his friends argued that gratitude to France, for her past support of the American Revolution, required that Americans should now support the French Revolution. Jefferson's opponents over this basic issue—of whom the most outspoken was the secretary of the treasury, Alexander Hamilton—firmly rejected that proposition. But they also realized the great emotional power that proposition exercised over millions of Americans, especially in the South. Hamilton and his friends, who had Washington's ear, were correspondingly suspicious of appeals to friendship with France and of gestures in line with such appeals. Madison's proposal in the House was certainly intended as such a gesture and was perceived as such in the Senate. Hence the Senate's adamant, and near-unanimous, refusal to follow suit.

French revolutionaries, of several different stripes, were now reaching out to the American Congress for support and getting support from the House of Representatives, but not from the Senate and not from the president. And Washington entrusted the handling of this episode not to his secretary of state but to his secretary of the treasury, Alexander Hamilton. As the editor of the monumental edition of Jefferson's letters, Julian P. Boyd, commented disapprovingly concerning the treatment of a key letter from Abbé Sieyès on behalf of the French National Assembly:

Yet the draft reply to Sieyès's letter was not proposed by the Secretary of State, who happened to possess a

personal knowledge of the leaders of the National Assembly, and who was highly respected by the moderates
among them. For that duty the President turned instead
to the Secretary of the Treasury, who had no first-hand
knowledge or experience of the revolutionary movement
in France, and who of course had no responsibility for
the conduct of foreign affairs.

But of course Washington didn't need or value Jefferson's firsthand knowledge or experience of the revolution
in France or need to rely on Hamilton for advice about
France. Washington had already, as early as October 13,
1789, made clear his personal assessment of the revolution in France, in his letter to his trusted friend, Gouverneur Morris. That assessment (quoted on pages 21–22)
was basically pessimistic, and decidedly penetrating in
its pessimism.

Washington knew of Jefferson's enthusiasm and
therefore did not trust Jefferson to handle negotiations
with French revolutionaries. He did trust Hamilton, and
rightly so. That is why he entrusted those delicate transactions with French revolutionaries to Hamilton and not
to Jefferson.

The friendship between Washington and Franklin,
formed certainly as early as the Constitutional Convention, had held firm into the last year of Franklin's life: "As

one of his last acts, Dr. Franklin had bequeathed a crab-tree walking-stick topped by a cap of liberty to 'my friend and the friend of mankind, General Washington. . . . If it were a scepter he has merited it and would become it.'"[9]

Washington was not treating Franklin himself in any derogatory fashion. He and Franklin had cooperated closely in the Constitutional Convention, and it is clear that they esteemed one another. What Washington was concerned about was a determined effort of two sets of French revolutionaries to exploit Franklin's memory in order to manipulate American sentiment and turn it into support for the French Revolution, thus involving America, if possible, in hostilities with Britain. Washington's refusal in the circumstances to sanction public mourning for Franklin has nothing to do with Franklin's personality, and everything to do with the protection of American neutrality.

IV

IN JULY 1790 CAME THE FIRST clear indication that the British government was positively inclined toward the conclusion of a treaty with the United States concerning which Washington had been sounding them, through his personal representative Gouverneur Morris, since October 1789:

> Memorandum of the substance of a Communication made on Thursday 8th July 1790 by Major Beckwith as by direction of Lord Dorchester [Britain's secretary of state for foreign affairs]: "That his Lordship had reason to believe that the Cabinet of Great Britain entertained a disposition not only towards a friendly intercourse but towards an alliance with the United States.[10]

This seems to be the first clear evidence of a positive response on the part of His Majesty's government to

Washington's informal overtures of more than a year earlier. Jefferson had not yet been informed by Washington of these soundings, and he still knew nothing about them. He heard about them only through a "leak" in late March 1791. The fact that Washington's secretary of the treasury knew all about these confidential negotiations but his secretary for foreign affairs did not is a sufficient indication of the relative degrees of confidence that Washington placed in these two Cabinet colleagues.

Washington's decision not to inform Jefferson of his own opening of negotiations, through Gouverneur Morris, for a treaty with Great Britain had been an overt if silent indication of his lack of confidence in his own secretary of state where relations with Britain were concerned. And this indication coincided with Jefferson's entering into the duties of his office.

As far as relations with revolutionary France were concerned, the first *overt* indication of Washington's lack of confidence in his secretary of state came when Washington committed a key negotiation with the French revolutionaries to his secretary of the treasury and not to the secretary of state, whose views were clear.

Early in January 1791, George Mason had written to Thomas Jefferson: "As I well know Your Attachment to the sacred Cause of Liberty must interest You in the

Success of the French Revolution, it is with great pleasure
I can inform You, that it is still going on prosperously."

In the following month, Jefferson replied to Mason,
relating "the Success of the French Revolution" and "the
sacred Cause of Liberty" specifically to the internal politics of the United States:

> I consider the establishment and success of their [French
> revolutionary] government as necessary to stay up our
> own and to prevent it from falling back to that kind of
> Half-way-house, the English constitution. It cannot be
> denied that we have among us a sect who believe that
> [English constitution] to contain whatever is perfect in
> human institutions; that the members of this sect have,
> many of them, names and offices which stand high in the
> estimation of our countrymen. I still rely that the great
> mass of our community is untainted with these heresies,
> as is its head.

The last four words have a rather hollow ring in the
context. George Washington may be "untainted" personally, but if he is, he is ineffective, since his government needs to be "stay[ed] up" by the "success" of the
French Revolution from "falling back" into that "Half-
way-house." And George Mason may well have won-

dered how it comes about that this untainted president keeps Alexander Hamilton, the heresiarch of the tainted sect, in his Cabinet and acquiesces in his Anglophile and otherwise suspect policies.

The exchange between Jefferson and Mason is illuminating with regard to the power of the French Revolution in American politics generally, and in Virginian politics in particular. Earlier, George Mason had been the intellectual leader of the antifederal side in the debates in Virginia over the Constitution and had thus been the adversary of the great Federalist James Madison, now Jefferson's chief ally. But over the French Revolution, these three Virginians are allies. The sacred cause of Liberty, identified with the success of the French Revolution, closes some past Virginian divisions (while threatening to open others, notably between Washington and the Jeffersonians) and opens up the attractive possibility of mobilizing "the great mass" of their "untainted" community against the heresies of a sect that happens to be most strongly established among the commercial and political classes of the Northeastern region of the United States.

Jefferson's biographers and editors often refer to such letters as this one to George Mason as "private letters." Yet there is nothing private about them. These are what were called in the eighteenth century "ostensible" letters:

letters meant to be shown to sympathizers. Through such letters, Jefferson was sending two simple, closely related messages to influential Virginians. The first message confirms Virginian suspicions of the federal government. The second shows that Thomas Jefferson, though a member of that government, is not corrupted by it, but still pure in heart and always vigilant in the cause of Liberty, Virginia, and the French Revolution.

The second example of Washington's lack of confidence in his secretary of state came on May 1791 with the publication of the American edition of Tom Paine's *Rights of Man*, an elegant commendation of the French Revolution. The edition carried a publisher's preface quoting a letter from the secretary of state, Thomas Jefferson, to Jonathan Bayard Smith, dated April 26, 1791, warmly praising Paine's book. The letter included these words: "He [Jefferson] is extremely pleased to find it will be re-printed here and that something is at length to be publicly said against the political heresies which have sprung up amongst us."

Five days later Jefferson wrote a letter to Washington claiming that his recommendation had been published "due to the indiscretion of a printer." He admitted that when he paid tribute to Paine's book and its salutary effects he had Adams in mind.

That I had in mind [John Adams's] *Discourses on Davila* is certain. But nothing was ever further from my thoughts than to become myself the contradictor before the public. To my great astonishment, however, when the pamphlet came out, the printer had prefixed my note to it, without having given me the most distant hint of it. Mr. Adams will unquestionably take to himself the charge of political heresy, as conscious of his own views of drawing the present government to the form of the English constitution and I fear will consider me as meaning to injure him in the public eye.

As Julian P. Boyd notes sadly: "To Jefferson's prompt and candid [*sic*] explanation of his note to Smith, Washington returned only an icy silence."[11] Boyd had hitherto tried to argue, against the weight of evidence, that Jefferson retained Washington's confidence. But that argument was no longer tenable. Boyd now comments:

The evidence is largely hidden in Washington's silence but, viewing the relation of the two men during the remainder of Jefferson's tenure as Secretary of State and over the ensuing years . . . it is difficult to escape the conclusion that the deterioration of the bonds of friendship, trust and affection that once existed between the central figure of the revolution and the pre-eminent spokesman for its moral and philosophical propositions had its origin in the unauthorized publication of Jefferson's letter to Jonathan Bayard Smith.[12]

In reality there is ample evidence, cited at length above, that Washington had never trusted his secretary of state in what concerned the most important matters falling within the secretary's mandate: relations with Great Britain and with revolutionary France.

Jefferson also wrote to John Adams trying to conciliate him. He wrote: "Indeed it was impossible that my note should occasion your name to be brought into question; for so far from naming you, I had not even in view any writing which I might suppose to be yours."

Jefferson here flatly contradicts what he had said to Washington, shortly before: "That I had in mind [Adams's] *Discourses on Davila* is certain."

Jefferson is usually pretty good at covering his tracks—which he did regularly—but now, under pressure, for a moment he loses his grip. What if Washington and Adams had compared notes of what Jefferson had told each of them separately?

Washington had good reasons of his own for not risking a public break with Jefferson. And, as would shortly appear, Jefferson too had good reasons of his own for not risking a public break with Washington.

The third and plainest example of the reasons for Washington's lack of confidence in his secretary of state, in the areas of relations with Britain and—especially—with revolutionary France, came with the secret foundation by Jefferson and Madison of a paper that would be a source of fierce attacks on President Washington (in whose Cabinet Jefferson was still serving) and equally fierce eulogies of the French Revolution and justifications of its massacres of French citizens. The vehicle became the *National Gazette*, and the editor appointed for it by Jefferson and Madison was Philip Freneau. Julian P. Boyd, who was in volume 20 of his monumental edition of the *Jefferson Papers* before showing signs of disillusion with Jefferson, whom he had so long praised and defended, thus described Freneau's qualifications for editing the *National Gazette*: "his own deep antipathy to the British people and their government, his uncritical acceptance of all propaganda favourable to the progress of the revolution in France, his hatred of monarchy and all its manifestations and his devotion to the principles of the American Revolution as he understood these."[13]

Boyd's list is accurate as far as it goes, but there are two important omissions: Freneau's bitter hostility to both President Washington and Alexander Hamilton. That hostility was encouraged by Washington's secretary of state, Thomas Jefferson, and (to a lesser extent) by Madison. Hamilton quickly saw what Jefferson was up to and challenged him pseudonymously but directly:

> Is it possible that Mr. Jefferson, the head of a principal department of the Government can be the Patron of a Paper, the evident object of which is to decry the Government and its measures? If he disapproves of the Government itself and thinks it deserving of opposition could he reconcile to his own personal dignity and the principles of probity to hold an office under it and employ the means of official influence in that opposition? If he disapproves of the leading measures . . . could he reconcile it with the principles of delicacy and propriety to continue to hold a place in that administration, and at the same time to be instrumental in nullifying measures which have been adopted by majorities of both branches of the Legislature and sanctioned by the *Chief Magistrate of the Union* [emphasis in the original]?[14]

Hamilton's charges against Jefferson were widely discussed, and little more than a month later Jefferson felt the need to issue a disclaimer to Washington. He admitted that he had supplied Freneau with copies of the (pro–French Revolution) *Gazette de Leide*, and then went on:

> But as to any other direction or indication of my wish how his press should be conducted, what sort of intelligence he should give, what essays encourage, I can protest in the presence of heaven, that I never did by myself or any other, directly or indirectly, say a syllable nor attempt any kind of influence.[15]

I have found that whenever Thomas Jefferson "protests in the presence of heaven" or "declares before God," he is certain to be lying. Jefferson went on:

> I can further protest, in the same awful presence, that I never did by myself or any other, directly or indirectly, write, dictate or procure any one sentence or sentiment to be inserted in his, or any other gazette to which my name was not affixed, or that of my office.[16]

Frank L. Mott's book *Jefferson and the Press* contains a chapter of commentary aptly entitled "Sub Rosa." In this, Mott writes:

Jefferson apparently attempted to keep his readers in this chess game of counter influences—his efforts at vote-getting, his play of one man against another, his management of both public and personal pressures—under cover and secret. Few public men have ever been more industrious letter-writers, and much of his correspondence was punctuated by pleas of secrecy. It is as though he felt a certain dichotomy in his political career—a cleavage between the Jefferson of history, and, on the other hand, Jefferson the political manager, whose smaller intrigues, necessary though they seemed at the time, were more or less distasteful and might better be private and easily forgotten.[17]

Julian P. Boyd, for so long a staunch defender of Jefferson, is constrained to agree substantially, though regretfully, with Mott:

The impression Jefferson sought to give the President—and his defenders to convince the public—that the appointment and the founding of the paper were unrelated is not persuasive. Considering the nominal duties given to the translating clerk and the highly disproportionate compensation he received, it can scarcely be denied that Jefferson had in fact offered, and Freneau had accepted, what can only be described as a political sinecure.[18]

The passage quoted above from Boyd is not an isolated one. Having described Madison's extensive contributions to the *National Gazette*, Boyd went on: "The contributions made by Jefferson to the *National Gazette*, despite the solemn assurance given to the President that he had never written or procured a single sentence for it, were more varied and extensive than those of Madison."

V

IN JANUARY 1792, the secretary of state informed Gouverneur Morris that the president's decision to nominate him as minister plenipotentiary to France had been approved by the Senate. This was another mark of Washington's lack of confidence in Jefferson in matters pertaining to the French Revolution. Charles T. Cullen—Boyd's successor as editor of the Jefferson papers—writes:

> Morris's nomination to succeed Jefferson as Minister to France came as a distinct shock and surprise to the Secretary of State. Washington decided on this nomination without consulting Jefferson beforehand and remained adamant in the face of an effort by Jefferson to persuade him to despatch Thomas Pinckney to Paris instead. Morris's nomination was a source of great unease to Jefferson because of the aristocratic New Yorker's well-known contempt for the French Revolution.[19]

We know that Thomas Pinckney despised George Washington. Jefferson seems to have known that he did, and that is probably why he recommended him.

Washington was of course well aware of Morris's attitude toward the French Revolution, which Washington himself shared. As Washington was later to intimate to Jefferson personally: "The letters of Gouverneur Morris give a gloomy picture of the affairs of France, I fear with too much truth." That is precisely why Washington appointed Morris to Paris and ignored Jefferson's protests and contrary advice.[20]

Yet Washington also had to be a bit careful how he handled Jefferson. When the House reacted overenthusiastically to the news of the king's ratification of the new French Constitution, Washington was at first inclined not to send on the House's message to Paris. "Washington softened his stand, however, after Jefferson advised him that support for the French Revolution was so widespread in America that few people would view the House's action as an encroachment on presidential authority."[21]

VI

ON MAY 9, 1792, Washington wrote to Hamilton, his
secretary of the treasury, authorizing him to execute the
act entitled "An Act to incorporate the subscription to
the Bank of the United States."

This was another bitter pill to Jefferson, and all the
more so as he himself had helped to open the political
way to the fulfillment of Hamilton's most cherished project. Shortly after Jefferson had taken office as secretary of
state, Jefferson and Madison had struck a bargain with
Hamilton. The deal was that if Hamilton supported a
favorite project of the two Virginians—the choice of a site
on the Potomac for the future capital of the United
States—the Virginians would allow Hamilton's bank safe
passage through Congress.

Once the two Virginian politicians had secured their
part of the bargain, and the planning of the capital on the
Potomac began, the two Virginians began bitterly to

regret the price they had paid for it, and Hamilton emerged as the principal target for the Republican Party's very active spokesmen in the press.

The foundation of the Bank of the United States was yet another great matter on which Washington and Hamilton cooperated, and, unlike the other major political issues, this was one on which Hamilton took the lead. Hamilton had studied economic matters long and carefully, and Washington had not. But Washington had carefully studied Hamilton's brief and became convinced that it fitted in with Washington's own policy for the security and greatness of the United States. He therefore came down in favor of the Bank of the United States, which enabled the bank to come into being, greatly to the advantage of the United States.

Great as Hamilton's influence was with Washington's first administration—and great as it continued to be after Hamilton had become a private citizen and confidential adviser to Washington—Hamilton's influence came to be exaggerated, not only by his enemies—of whom Jefferson was the chief organizer—but also by Hamilton's admirers. Thus Joseph Charles writes of the Massachusetts Federalist Timothy Pickering:

> Timothy Pickering was one of the men who tried to exploit Washington's prestige but who did not regard him

highly except in a moral sense. Years after Washington's death he wrote: "No man, however well-informed, was willing to hazard his own popularity by exhibiting the real intellectual character of the immensely popular Washington." He thought that Washington's prudence and want of decision had been due to his realization of his own deficiencies and that while it was patriotic for those who were aware of his defects to have been silent on this point, so as not to undermine public confidence, there was no reason why they should remain silent longer. "But who originated the great measures of Washington's administration? Certainly not Washington." Pickering gave Hamilton almost all of the credit and thought that if it had not been for Hamilton, Jefferson would have had an influence with Washington similar to that which Hamilton exerted.[22]

Most of Pickering's analysis, quoted above, is pretty shaky, and the conclusion is demonstrably false. We know now that Washington, before Jefferson joined his Cabinet, had reached conclusions on Britain and revolutionary France, which were to lead years later to a treaty with Britain and a break with revolutionary France. Jefferson disapproved of all that but was unable to prevent it.

Hamilton approved of Washington's policies toward France and Britain and ably abetted them, but there is no evidence that he helped to shape them. Washington's own powerful and original political capacity is amply evident, especially in his early, brilliant, and accurate analysis of where the French Revolution was headed.

Washington was never glib, and he was often reserved and sometimes cryptic in his public pronouncements. He therefore tended to be underestimated by glib little men. And poor Pickering was an outstanding example of a glib little man.

VII

ON MAY 23, 1792, Jefferson wrote an exceptionally long and earnest letter, containing a kind of remonstrance, to George Washington. The letter contains not a syllable of direct reference to the French Revolution but is of great importance with regard to the context—in particular, the response surveys the early 1790s. Jefferson's letter opens with a respectful plea, and one that seems to imply that Washington had been keeping him at a distance in the early part of the year:

> I have determined to make the subject of a letter, what, for some time past, has been a subject of inquietude to my mind without having found a good occasion of disburthening itself to you in conversation, during the busy scenes which occupied you here. Perhaps too you may be able, in your present situation, or on the road, to give it

more time and reflection than you could do here at any moment.

When you first mentioned to me your purpose of retiring from the government, tho' I felt all the magnitude of the event, I was in a considerable degree silent. I knew that, to such a mind as yours, persuasion was idle and impertinent: that before forming your decision, you had weighed all the reasons for and against the measure, had made up your mind on full view of them, and that there could be little hope of changing the result. Pursuing my reflections too I knew we were some day to try to walk alone, and if the essay should be made while you should be alive and looking on, we should derive confidence from that circumstance, and resource if it failed. The public mind too was then calm and confident, and therefore in a favorable state for making the experiment. Had no change of circumstances supervened, I should not, with any hope of success, have now ventured to propose to you a change of purpose. But the public mind is no longer so confident and serene; and that from causes in which you are no ways personally mixed.

The adverb *personally*, in that last sentence, is crucial. For the "causes," which Jefferson goes on to denounce at length, consist of nothing less than the whole financial policy of Washington's first administration. The policy was being carried out by Alexander Hamilton, but without Washington's approval, Hamilton would not be secretary of the treasury. So the word *personally* is a polite fiction. While pleading with Washington to serve for a second term—lest worse befall, perhaps John Adams—Jefferson is obliquely telling Washington that he detests almost all the important things that have been done during Washington's first term.

Jefferson's charges against the Hamiltonian system need not be detailed here. They are standard Republican stuff and, as Jefferson himself acknowledges to Washington, "hackneyed in the public press." The part of this letter that is most relevant to our present study is the warning that the inflammation of sectional differences may lead to a civil war:

> But the division of sentiment and interest happens unfortunately to be so geographical, that no mortal can say that what is most wise and temperate would prevail against what is more easy and obvious. I can scarcely contemplate a more incalculable evil than the breaking of the union into two or more parts. Yet when we review the mass which opposed the original coalescence, when we consider that it lay chiefly in the Southern quarter, that the legislators have availed themselves of no occa-

sion of allaying it, but on the contrary whenever Northern and Southern prejudices have come into conflict, the
latter have been sacrificed and the former soothed; that
the owers of the debt are in the Southern and the holders
of it are in the Northern division; that the Antifederal
champions are now strengthened in argument by the ful-
filment of their predictions; that this has been brought
about by the Monarchial federalists themselves, who,
having been for the new government merely as a step-
ping stone to monarchy, have themselves adopted the
very constructions of the constitution, of which, when
advocating its acceptance before the tribunal of the
people, they declared it insusceptible; that the republican federalists [Jefferson is clearly referring to Madison],
who espoused the same government for its intrinsic merits, are disarmed of their weapons, that which they denied as prophecy being now become true history: who
can not be sure that these things may not proselyte the
small number which was wanting to place the majority
on the other side? And this is the event at which I trem-
ble, and to prevent which I consider your continuance at
the head of affairs as of the last importance. The confidence of the whole nation is centered in you. You being at
the helm, will be more than an answer to every argument
which can be used to alarm the people in any quarter
into violence or secession. North and South will hang

together, if they have you to hang on: and, if the first cor-
rective of a numerous representation should fail in its effect, your presence will require time for trying others not
inconsistent with the union and the peace of the states.

Jefferson was, at this time, busy fanning that same
Southern resentment (against Northern hegemony)
about the power of which he is warning Washington. Of
the attacks on Hamilton's policies (which were also
Washington's) Charles T. Cullen quaintly observed,
"This critique had been taking shape in the pages of the
National Gazette since the beginning of 1792 and there
can be little doubt that TJ was influenced by that paper's
criticism of the underlying implications of the Secretary
of the Treasury's economic program."

But of course Jefferson and Madison had set up the
National Gazette precisely in order to *mount* the kind of
"critique" of Hamiltonian policy that Cullen innocently
supposes to have "influenced" Jefferson. It looks as if the
editor of volume 23 of *The Papers of Thomas Jefferson* had
never read the Editorial Note at the end of volume 20, in
which his predecessor, Julian P. Boyd, clearly sets out the
part the *National Gazette* was founded to play in the political strategies of Jefferson and Madison.

The exploitation of American enthusiasm for the
French Revolution was integral to that strategy. This was

an issue that united the (white) South (with a few exceptions) and tended to split the population of the North
along class lines. So the *National Gazette* played up the
French Revolution, and James Madison made adroit use
of it in the House of Representatives. Jefferson, as Washington's secretary of state, had to be more discreet, but he
was in reality the mastermind of the whole operation.

When Jefferson warned Washington about the danger of confronting the House over the French Revolution, he was speaking of the power of emotions that he
himself was doing more than any other American to keep
alive and inflamed. And Washington knew this.

Washington kept on Hamilton and continued to
support him, but Jefferson's plea—and, perhaps even
more, his warning—is believed to have been among the
factors that influenced Washington's decision to accept a
second term.

WASHINGTON IS NOT KNOWN TO have replied in writing, or indeed otherwise, to Jefferson's long letter of May
23, 1792. But he had strong reasons to consider it very
carefully indeed. There is ample reason (considered
above) to believe that Washington deeply distrusted Jefferson, primarily over relations with Britain and revolutionary France, but also over the American economy. For
instance: Jefferson's opposition to the Bank of the United

States, a Hamiltonian project of great importance for the future of the United States, which Washington had consistently approved and Jefferson, no less consistently, had sought to undermine, not openly, but through many agents loyal to him, in the political world and in the press.

Washington knew Jefferson as a committed and dangerous secret adversary. But he could also see that Jefferson could be even more dangerous, not merely to Washington but even to the existence of the United States, if Washington rebuffed him and then retired from the presidency. Jefferson would probably then be pitted against Adams electorally, and the contest would then be conducted along bitter regional lines between North and South. What would then loom would be the specter of civil war.

So Washington had strong reasons—national ones, transcending personal ones—for keeping Jefferson on board. And in this letter, Jefferson was offering to come on board and support Washington, if Washington ran for a second term as president of the United States. With Jefferson on board the Washington campaign train, foreign relations and the Bank of the United States— potentially the most explosive campaigning issues—would have to be kept on the back burner at least for the duration of the election campaign. No doubt they would reemerge during Washington's second term, but they would be deprived of most of their explosive character since Jefferson, and the whole of the Republican Party, following Jefferson, would have again endorsed the president.

Jefferson's own calculations were probably that if he challenged Adams for the presidency, and Adams was backed by Washington (even silently), Jefferson could not win. It was therefore in his interest to give Washington a second term without a fight.

Washington could see that, in the national interest, it was imperative for him to win a second term. During that term, the Bank of the United States, at the heart of America's growing prosperity, could establish itself still more firmly, and American foreign policy would remain in prudent hands. Thus American prosperity could be placed on a firmer basis. The specter of coming civil war could probably not be exorcised, granted the regional imbalances, but whenever the final struggle might come, if its outcome were postponed, the Southern secessionists would be so much the weaker party, in resources and in capacity, that they would have to lose, though perhaps in a long and bitter war.

So the election of President Washington for an uncontested second term was a nationally desirable objective in an important episode in the history of the United States.

WHY DID WASHINGTON RETAIN Jefferson as secretary of
state while he deeply distrusted him? He did so for two
reasons. Washington already feared what was to happen
more than half a century later: the secession of the Southern states from the Union. Jefferson was a pivotal figure
in the politics of Virginia, the most populous and richest
state in the South. Keeping Jefferson aboard, even if pre-
cariously, at least allowed the Union to gain some precious
time, in which it would be gaining strength and wealth to
face, if necessary, a long trial.

The situation was more crisply summed up by a
twentieth-century American politician, explaining why
he kept an obstreperous and treacherous colleague in
high office. Lyndon Baines Johnson's memorable answer
was: "It's better to have the man inside the tent, pissing
out, than outside the tent, pissing in."[23]

My friend Michael Williams, a subtle student of history as well as a political analyst, has written a most ingenious speech by a fictional Thomas Jefferson speaking
in his own defense. It is the best that anyone could do for
Jefferson, so let me end this section by quoting it in full,
without further comment.

I acknowledge that I lied to Adams, as my accuser says.

Has none of you ever told a social lie? What would
you do if in the course of expressing your own deeply

held convictions you had necessarily criticized the views of an old friend, and he seemed upset? Is it not a natural courtesy to deny any intention of attacking him personally? Even if your denial is not one hundred percent true, are you guilty of anything more than a polite falsehood, understood and even expected among courteous people?

My accuser makes much of this minor transgression, if indeed transgression it was. I will come back to this shortly and ask you to consider what light this casts on his own motives.

As regards the re-issue of the "Rights of Man," Julian Boyd, with some expertise in the area, has described my explanation as "prompt and candid." I accept that description. But while I stand over my statement that I did not intend my comments on Paine's word to be published, I would not feel guilt or shame if I had publicly endorsed what I consider to be a great work that so eloquently and rationally expressed my convictions.

My accuser makes much of the National Gazette, and my alleged support for it. Well, as a person accused, I am entitled to remain silent and require my accuser to prove his case, while I claim the benefit of the doubt. But let me ask, if I did support Freneau as editor, would that be something of which I should be ashamed?

Freneau and I shared the same—I was going to say views but that is too feeble a word—we shared the same convictions. I entered political life, and remained active in politics in pursuit of my convictions. Indeed, I accepted Washington's invitation to serve under him as his Secretary of State in the belief that the invitation signaled that he would be a genuinely non-partisan President and my role would enable me to have some influence in guiding my country in the direction I believed to be best for it and the rest of struggling mankind.

Was it wrong for me to support a journal that advanced views I believed in?

My accuser says that while it might be acceptable for a private citizen to support an anti-Government paper, it was unacceptable for a serving Secretary of State to do so. In general, that may be valid, but, as the accusations leveled against me show, my position was not that of a normal Secretary, serving a normal President. Having been invited to serve by a President who well knew and understood my convictions, I reasonably expected to be part of a non-partisan Administration, and that during my tenure of that Office I might advance at least some of the causes to which I had dedicated my energies. (Washington did not ask me to suspend my convictions while serving, or to go against them in serving him. He knew me well enough not to make me so insulting an offer.)

After I had served him for over a year, I discovered, by chance and in spite of his continuous attempts at concealment, that while retaining me in that office he had deliberately by-passed me in pursuing a policy hidden from me, of seeking to forge an alliance with my country's inveterate enemy. Not only that, but he had engaged in a conspiracy with other people, including people nominally my subordinates, to hide his activities from me.

A Secretary of State who supports an anti-Government paper would normally be accused of acting disloyally. Jurors! Let me invite you, before you convict me of disloyalty, to ask of yourselves a few questions. Such as: Is the duty of loyalty a one-way thoroughfare, owed only by the subordinate, or does it run two ways? Was Washington's conduct towards me, as I have described it above, loyal to me? Did I owe loyalty to a President who had set himself to subvert the Office which he had entrusted to me, to hide from its holder activities he might rationally consider treasonous to our country, to mislead him, and to conspire with his subordinates in doing so? Was this the conduct of a man "just, humane, temperate and sincere"? Or "uniform"? Or "edifying to all around him"?

I must now enter an even graver aspect of my defense by requesting you to ask yourselves why Washington requested me to serve as his Secretary of State?

Is it not clear that at the time he extended this invitation to me, he had embarked on a course he knew I would feel it my duty to oppose? Look at the dates! His letter to Gouverneur Morris inviting him to ascertain whether a British treaty might be negotiated is dated October 1789. He invited me to serve him as Secretary of State on 21 January 1790. And he said not a word about a British Treaty to the person he asked to act as his Secretary of State at the time of the invitation, or when I agreed to serve, or when I took office, or at any time thereafter! On the contrary he pursued a course of double-dealing and concealment. From the very beginning, and throughout my tenure of the Office, his course was marked with falsehood and duplicity.

Ask yourselves why. Why did he seek to link Thomas Jefferson to his Administration? It is not easy to read the mind of so devious a man, but I can give you two reasons I think to be plausible. First is he knew that as a private citizen I would have opposed these secret treaty negotiations as soon as they came to light, so he hoped to neutralize my opposition by making me part of his "team."

But I believe he had a second and more sinister motive. If the treaty had been finalized and announced during my tenure of office, my friends and supporters would have repudiated not just the Treaty but me as the Secretary of State during whose tenure of that Office it had been negotiated.

Thus, Jurors, I conceive this devious unscrupulous man aimed, with elegant economy, to achieve two objectives by bringing me into his Cabinet and hiding its activities from me: to neutralize my anticipated opposition to his treasonous plan to join our ancient enemy in a treaty of friendship hostile to our greatest and most valued ally; and to bring about the political ruin of his leading opponent.

I ask you again: did I owe loyalty to such a man?

Some of you may say it would have been more open and manly on my part to have resigned from the Washington Cabinet as soon as his duplicity was uncovered. And I tell you frankly that was my instinct—even when my anger and indignation had cooled somewhat. But I had to consider the good of my country, and ask myself how best to serve it. And ask myself whether it might not be better for my country that I fight fire with fire, duplicity with duplicity.

Before I close, let me explain why I ignore comments with which this text is studded about my "devious temperament," my being "good at covering my tracks" and the like. I do so because I believe such unsupported accusations indict the accuser, not the accused.

Finally, Jurors, before you go to the room in which you will consider and decide my guilt or innocence, let me ask you to consider not just the nature of the accusations brought against me, and the character of my accuser. Notoriously, he is an enemy of the Revolution in France and those who support and supported it, and a friend of those who opposed it. Chief among whom I count Burke and Washington.

I do not question his honesty in rejecting the Revolution. Let him not question mine in supporting it. I believe that in spite of its excesses (which I regret, but which as a politician of the day I was bound to overlook so far as I could and to minimize in my public utterances) the Revolution in France was a giant step forward for mankind, not, as my accuser believes, a retrograde step.

My accuser can see no wrong in those who share his view, and no virtue in those who do not. As an example of this, remember his excitement about the social lie I acknowledge I told Adams, to spare his feelings. I ask you to conclude not only that my accuser sees clearly whatever mote may be in my eye, and even some that may not be there, but that he ignores the beam that I submit an unbiased reading of his indictment will show in Washington's.

•

I don't agree with the negative observations on Washington, but I do concede that this is about the best case that can reasonably be made for Jefferson.

Part Two

WASHINGTON'S
SECOND TERM

I

ON MARCH 4, 1793, Washington, having been reelected without a contest, delivered his second inaugural
address:

Fellow Citizens; I am again called upon by the voice of
my country to execute the functions of its chief magis-
trate. When the occasion proper for it shall arrive I shall
endeavour to express the high sense I entertain of this
distinguished honour, and of the confidence which has
been reposed in me by the people of the United States.

Previous to the execution of any official act of the
President, the Constitution requires an oath of office. This
oath I am now about to take in your presence, that if it
shall be found during my administration of the government I have in any instance violated willingly or dis-
obeyed the injunction thereof, I may (besides incurring

Constitutional punishment) be subject to the upbraidings of all who are now witnesses of the present ceremony.

Having quoted the full text, as set out above, of Washington's second inaugural address, Washington's biographer, James Thomas Flexner, immediately goes on to comment:

> Having spoken soberly of duty and punishment, Washington took the oath and retired as quickly and unobtrusively as possible to his residence. He was committed to four more years of what he angrily described as "slavery."[1]

Having strongly urged Washington to accept a second term, Jefferson would probably have wanted the occasion of Washington's installation as president to pass without immediate adverse comment. But the forces Jefferson had helped to set in motion from behind the scenes had by now acquired a momentum of their own. The *National Gazette*, edited by Jefferson's protégé and employee Philip Freneau, immediately stated that "the monarchical farce of the birthday" had been deployed with "*great* exertions" by sinister persons for sinister purposes. And he added, "Hitherto, the people have passed over the absurdities of *levees* [Washington's official afternoon receptions] *and every species of royal pomp and parade* because they were associated with the man of their affections . . . but their own interest has at length conquered the delicacy of their attachment and they begin to express the abhorrence of the capers of a court with the manliness of freemen who are resolved not to erect a funeral pyre for their liberties." Washington was cherishing a "set of vipers . . . who, animated by too indulgent warmth, have struck their poisonous fangs into the placid bosom of peace and virtue."[2]

The contributors to the *National Gazette* (or the editor, under a pseudonym) kept up the running fire. Thus a letter signed simply by "A Farmer" warned that if the public continued to set up Washington as an "idol," he might well, "over the prostrate body of the citizens," establish a dictatorship.

II

In April 1793, Jean-Baptiste Ternant, minister plenipotentiary of the French Republic to the United States, was
in Philadelphia, awaiting the arrival of his successor, Citizen Edmond-Charles Genêt. On April 18, Ternant reported to the citizen minister of foreign affairs of the
republic:

> The President is back here [from Mount Vernon, to
> Philadelphia] since yesterday—the English war [with
> France] is giving more and more concern to the Ameri-
> can Government, and I have reason to believe that it is
> about to proclaim its neutrality; on the basis of the press
> reports that war has broken out [*sur la seule notoriété de
> la guerre*] and without waiting for official notification
> from the belligerent powers. The extreme probability of
> such a position of the United States, in such a case, was
> reported in several of my former dispatches [which had

been unanswered]. I am greatly distressed [*jugez si je dois souffrir*] to be left without information with regard to future French policy towards America [*le parti que la France veut adopter relativement à l'Amérique*]. Also at seeing that my successor, although nominated last November, is still not at his post on April 18—I have pledged myself to remain at my post, and I shall keep that pledge faithfully, but as soon as I am released by the arrival of Citizen Genêt I hope I shall have sufficient resolve, despite my extreme poverty, never again to be the agent of any Government whatever [*ne plus être l'agent d'aucun gouvernement quelconque*].

Jean-Baptiste Ternant had reason to be sick at heart. His life had been a diplomatic misery since news of the events of August 1792 had reached America, toward the end of the same year. Ternant had served in the American Revolution, under Steuben, and on his appointment as minister plenipotentiary (August 1791) had been recommended to Washington by Lafayette. Washington had regarded him as "an old friend." But a year later to be known as a friend of Lafayette was to be in deep disgrace with the authorities in Paris. Among the Girondins, *Fayettiste* was the worst possible term of opprobrium. (We shall see below how this term was to be applied by Ternant's successor to Washington himself.)

The best that Ternant could look forward to, had he returned to France, was a life of provincial obscurity; the
guillotine was a distinct possibility. So he stayed on in
America (as his successor was also to do). Ternant lived
until 1816.

On April 20, Ternant wrote again to his citizen minister, this time to announce the arrival of his successor in
the United States, but not in the capital, to which he was
accredited. Ternant wrote, with exasperation:

> A ship from Charleston has finally brought me a letter
> dated 11th. of this month in which Citizen Genêt an-
> nounces his arrival in that city, and his immediate depar-
> ture for Philadelphia. It will take him at least 22 days to
> make that wearisome journey; and as he probably left on
> the 12th, I can't expect to see him here until the opening
> days of May. It is much to be regretted, since he is en-
> trusted, as he says himself, with important negotiations,
> that he should have taken the longest possible route
> to reach the place in which these negotiations have to
> be conducted.

Actually, Genêt spent eleven days in Charleston, and
twenty-nine days en route, reaching Philadelphia on
May 16. This was a deliberate progress for a set purpose:

to excite, display, and exploit American enthusiasm for the French Revolution. This was no ordinary diplomatic mission, from one government to another. This was a mission from one nation to another; from one people to another; from one republic to another; from one revolution to another. Meeting the people was more important than meeting the president. So Genêt took his time and met the people. The general idea was that the president—usually referred to by Genêt simply as General Washington—would be more receptive of Citizen Genêt's message from the French Republic, after Washington had witnessed the enthusiasm of his own people for Citizen Genêt, and for the French Revolution incarnate in the person of the citizen.

Jefferson and Madison were later to have cause to deplore Genêt's manner of appealing to the people, but they were delighted with his initial progress. On April 28, 1793, Jefferson wrote to Madison: "We expect Mr. Genêt here within a few days. It seems as if his arrival would furnish occasion for the *people* to testify their affections without respect to the cold cautions of their government." This is of course precisely what Genêt intended. The meeting of minds, across great distances, is remarkable, at this stage of the Genêt-Jefferson interaction. On May 29, Madison is eager for publication of Genêt's addresses.

The sentiments expressed by Genêt would be of infinite service at this crisis. As a regular publication of them cannot be expected till the meeting of Congress, if then, it will be wished they could in some other mode make their way to the press. If he expressed the substance of them in his verbal answer to the address, or announces them in open conversation, the Printers might surely hand them to the public. The affection to France in her struggles for liberty would not only be increased by a knowledge that she does not wish us to go to war; but prudence would give its sanction to a bolder enunciation of the popular sentiment.

At this stage, then, Jefferson and Madison regarded Genêt's arrival as constituting a most valuable reinforcement for the American Republican cause. They were in a mood to egg him on. But they were soon to find that egging on was not exactly what Citizen Genêt required.

Genêt was, personally, a most attractive advocate of his cause: young, handsome, dashing, outgoing, sincerely eloquent; a romantic representative of the French Revolution in its most romantic phase. Women fell in love with him, at the mere sound of his approach. The lady whom he was to marry—Cornelia, daughter of Governor George Clinton of New York—let it be known that she was in love with him before ever she set eyes on

him, just on the strength of what she heard about him, as
he journeyed north from Charleston.

Arousing popular enthusiasm was the most essential
part of Citizen Genêt's mission, and he was extremely
good at this. But his mission also involved more practical
activities, and he set about these energetically from the
moment of his arrival in Charleston. Harry Ammon writes:

> Within a few days after his arrival, Genêt commissioned
> four privateers. Christened most appropriately, *Republi-
> can, Anti-George, Sans-Culotte,* and—the finest touch of
> all—*Citizen Genêt,* they were soon sending into Charles-
> ton English ships captured as prizes. The Minister also
> made the initial arrangements for an expedition to be
> launched against Spanish Florida. The details of this oper-
> ation were entrusted to the French Consul, Michel Ange
> Mangourit, whose patriotism met Genêt's approval.

Ammon says that Genêt took these steps while "totally ignorant of the administration's position." But
Genêt was not "totally ignorant" of this. He knew the administration's position very well, *as the position was represented in the Republican press,* of which the bellwether
was Jefferson's *National Gazette.* For more than a year
before Genêt's mission began, those French revolutionaries who were interested in America had been receiving

through that press the Jeffersonian picture of Washington's first administration. Genêt's chief, and Jefferson's old acquaintance, Brissot de Warville, was thoroughly familiar with that picture. Washington's administration—as the Republican press could tell you—contained one good man, whose heart and soul was with the French Revolution. This was Thomas Jefferson. It also contained one bad man, in the pay of the king of England. This was Alexander Hamilton. Then there was Washington, a good man but unaccountably open to the evil influence of Hamilton. Since 1791, French diplomatic representatives had been taken into Jefferson's confidence in these matters. So it was not that Genêt was totally ignorant of the administration's position. He knew that position, in the Republican version of it, and that is what Genêt, with the approval of the Republican leaders, wanted to change. He was confident that it could be changed, when he had demonstrated the extent of the power that the French Revolution possessed over the hearts and minds of the American people.

Citizen Genêt was not an ignorant blunderer, as he has sometimes been represented. He was a revolutionary, acting consistently on revolutionary premises. He didn't, as a revolutionary, need the permission of the American administration for any project he might undertake on behalf of the French Revolution. What he needed was the permission of a superior power: the American people, who were held to be heart and soul with the French people. For Citizen Genêt, as for other revolutionaries, "the people" always meant those people who were on the side of the revolution; the others didn't count. So the plaudits of the people of Charleston constituted a fully adequate mandate for military action in Charleston Harbor. If Washington's administration were to contest the legitimacy of that act, it would be revealing its own lack of legitimacy because it would be going against the source of all legitimacy: the people. This was not only sound revolutionary logic in a general way. It was specifically the logic and the modus operandi of the French Revolution in all its phases, as Burke had known as early as September 1789. By mobilizing "the people" against the executive, the ancien régime had been destroyed. In August 1792, the constitutional monarchy had been destroyed by the same revolutionary logic and the same methods. And in June 1793—the month after Citizen Genêt's arrival in Philadelphia—the Girondin version of the republic was to be swept away by Robespierre's Jacobins, and the people would mark Genêt's friends for the guillotine. But neither Genêt nor Washington's administration learned of those developments until near the end of 1793, by which time Genêt's mission was coming to an end anyway; for American reasons, not French ones.

It came later to be maintained by Republicans that Genêt had exceeded the instructions he received from France's Executive Council of the Girondin regime. The French Revolution was absolutely all right, as always. It was one misguided individual, the regrettable Edmond-Charles Genêt, who was alone responsible for everything that had gone wrong in the relations between America and France in the summer of 1793. That was the retrospective thesis that came to be adopted by Jefferson and the Republicans. That Genêt had exceeded his instructions became a Republican article of faith. So let us take a look at the instructions in question. The passages that follow are my own translation.

The first thing to note about the instructions is the capacity (*qualité*) in which Genêt is to act. He is described as "Minister Plenipotentiary of the French Republic to [*près*] the Congress of the United States." Harry Ammon described this as "a minor error, which reflected the Girondin vagueness about American institutions." I don't think this is either minor or an error. Brissot de Warville, at this time the leading figure among the Girondins, had made a study of American affairs and must have known, at least in outline, of the system of government established by the American Constitution, by now in operation for more than three years. There is vagueness here, but it is calculated vagueness, *revolutionary* vagueness. The institutions of other countries were perceived on behalf of the French Republic as legitimate only in the degree that they resembled the pan-revolutionary archetype: the French Republic, One and Indivisible. In that respect Congress had legitimacy, through its resemblance to the National Convention. On the other hand, the idea of a chief executive, elected by the people, had no analogue in French revolutionary terms and therefore no revolutionary legitimacy. The form of accreditation of Citizen Genêt is certainly mistaken *in American terms.* But it is not at all mistaken *in French revolutionary terms.* In appealing to Congress, over the head of the president (as he was soon to do) Citizen Genêt was acting, not only in accordance with the letter of his instructions, but also with their spirit. And also with the spirit of the French Revolution, which was a strongly nationalist spirit and never more profoundly nationalist than when, as under the Girondins, it abounded in the rhetoric of the most exalted *internationalism.*

In that spirit, Genêt will appeal to Congress against the executive, and he will continue to accredit consuls to Congress, even after the American executive has instructed him to refrain from doing so. This is not a series

of personal blunders: it is the unfolding of revolutionary policy.

The opening paragraph of Genêt's instructions makes
clear that he is expected to be not just an envoy accredited to a governmental institution but also, and primarily, a revolutionary missionary to the American people.
Having referred to the links that unite "the French Nation" to "the American People," the instructions require
Citizen Genêt "to devote his energies to fortifying the
Americans in the Principles which have induced them
[*les ont engages*] to unite themselves to France."

Genêt would not have needed to be told that "fortifying" the Americans in these "Principles" included instructing them on what those principles actually were.
This was standard, both in doctrine and practice, during
the ideologically expansionist phases of the French Revolution, the most exuberant of these phases being that of
the Girondins in 1793.

The French Revolution schema of a legitimate American political system, united with the French one, is perfectly clear. The American administration is legitimate
only if its members regard themselves as "Ministers of
Congress" and behave as such. Congress itself is legitimate only if it shows itself as "obedient to the will of the
people." The envoy of the French Revolution, applauded
and thereby accredited by the American people, is ipso

facto constituted arbiter of the legitimacy or illegitimacy
of both ministers and Congress. It is implicit in the logic
of the instructions, and of the revolution from which
they emanate, that if Congress and its supposed "ministers" fail to comply with the directives conveyed to them
by the envoy of the French Revolution, a new American
Revolution will be in order, to be conducted on French
revolutionary lines.

Citizen Genêt is to seek to develop previous negotiations for a commercial treaty into something far more
ambitious and revolutionary: "a national pact in which
the two peoples would completely combine [*confon-
draient*] their commercial interests with their political interests and establish an intimate concert [*concert intime*]
in order to promote [*favoriser*] in all connections [*sous
tous les rapports*] the Empire of Liberty."

The words *national pact* deserve comment. Within
the "intimate concert" of "the Empire of Liberty" are
America and France to become *one nation*? It might seem
so, but if that is the case, the momentous fusion is not to
take place immediately, for the "national pact" is to require that the ships of certain powers are "not to be
received in the ports of the two contracting Nations" (as
the powers in question are clearly meant to include
Britain, this part of Genêt's instructions would have auto-
matically involved the United States in war with Britain).

Warming to their work, the members of the Executive Council go on to describe how the Empire of Liberty might be made up, territorially speaking, under the binational "national pact":

> The pact, which the French People would support with all the characteristic energy of which it has already furnished so many proofs, would lead rapidly to the liberation of Spanish America, would open the navigation of the Mississippi, would deliver our brothers-of-old [*anciens frères*] from the tyrannical yoke of Spain, and perhaps reunite to the American Constellation the beautiful star of Canada. However vast this project may be, it will be easy to execute, if the Americans want it, and Citizen Genêt must devote himself to encouraging them to do so.

The passage about the Empire of Liberty is followed by one in which the reasons for France's declaration of war on "the King of England" are explained. The formula is a classic of French revolutionary thinking and does much to explain both the conduct and the eventual failure of Citizen Genêt's mission to the United States. The relevant passage in the instructions was:

> The English Ministers, instead of associating themselves with the glory of France, instead of realizing that

our liberty, as well as that of the Peoples whose chains we have broken, guarantees Forever [à *Jamais*] that of their Country [*Patrie*] allow themselves to be influenced by our enemies, who are also those of the Liberty of Peoples.

Note the implications: that other nations yearn to be associated with the glory of France, implicitly superior to anything the other nations may possess of their own in that line; also that other nations would be content to have their liberty "guaranteed" for them by France (and defined for them by their guarantor) rather than to have their liberty cherished and defended by themselves, in their own way and on their own terms.

Those numerous Americans who admired the French Revolution, or what they thought of as the French Revolution, would hardly have been happy with that formulation, if they had known about it and been able to ponder its implications for themselves.

The instructions conclude by instructing their minister plenipotentiary about matters of protocol and precedence. In the earlier part, and in a general context, the instructions had spoken of "flinging away far from us everything that pertains to the old Diplomacy." In the concluding part, it is made clear that the rejection of the "old Diplomacy" does not apply to the precedence to which a diplomatic representative of France was traditionally entitled (i.e., under the defunct ancien régime). Having told Citizen Genêt to avoid "the ridiculous disputes which took up the time of the old Diplomacy," the Executive Council explains how he is to conduct himself, as minister plenipotentiary of France (as well as of the republic) should any such dispute arise. There is a general policy to be followed by all ministers of the French Republic in such cases:

> The intent of the Council is that the Ministers of the Nation declare openly and proudly [*hautement*] that the French People sees in all the Peoples brothers and equals, and that it wishes to set aside [*écarter*] all idea of supremacy and precedence, but that if any State, misunderstanding the generosity of [French revolutionary] principles, were to claim any special distinction, and were to put itself in a position to acquire such a thing by direct or indirect diplomatic representations [*demarches*], the Ministers of the French People would then demand all the prerogatives enjoyed in every time by the French power [*la puissance Française*], the Nation being determined that, in such a case, its Ministers defend these prerogatives, in the knowledge that She [*Elle, la Nation*] will know how to ensure that they are respected [*les faire respecter*].

In short, all Peoples are equal, but some Peoples are more equal than others.

The above are the principal promises contained in the main body of the Executive Council's far-reaching instructions to the revolutionary plenipotentiary to the United States. But there is also a "supplement" to the instructions, which is even more illuminating than the main body of this document with regard to French revolutionary attitudes to the United States, in the epoch of maximum French revolutionary ideological expansion (1793).

The supplement begins by acknowledging that the minister plenipotentiary, in attempting to carry out his instructions, may run into American resistance, at a high level (or what would have been regarded as a high level before the advent of the doctrine of the supremacy of the people). The first paragraph of the supplement runs:

> The Executive Council wishes a new treaty, on wider and more fraternal foundations than those of 1778, to be concluded as soon as possible. However, the Council has to recognize that during the present crisis of Europe a negotiation of this nature may be subject to many delays whether as a result of secret maneuvers of the [British] Minister and the English partisans at Philadelphia or because of the timidity of several leaders of the American Republic who, despite their well-known patriotism,

have always shown the strongest aversion for any measures which could mean the displeasure of England.

Always? Even during the American Revolution? Yes,
apparently, for the Executive Council goes on to tell its
plenipotentiary the argument by which he is to overcome
the timidity of George Washington and his colleagues:

> He will make the Americans realize that the engage-
> ments which may appear onerous to them are no more
> than the just price of *the independence which the French
> Nation won for them* [emphasis mine] and the more se-
> vere he shows himself to be on these points, the more
> easy it will be to induce them to conclude a new Treaty.

Citizen Genêt has often been accused of exceeding
his instructions, but he fell well short of them in this
particular. This was prudent on his part. Had he insisted
on explaining to the crowds that came out to meet him on
the road from Charleston to Philadelphia in that month of
May that the Americans owed their liberation, not in any
degree to their own exertions and sacrifices, but entirely
to the French nation, the representative of the nation in
question might never have reached Philadelphia alive.

The enthusiasm of Jefferson and Madison for the
French Revolution would have been sensibly abated had

they known that in the authoritative opinion of the Executive Council of the French Republic, Americans must be grateful and pay for "the independence which the French Nation won for them." It was, of course, a standard theme of American Republican oratory that Americans should be grateful for the support the French had given to the American Revolution, and that the Federalists were ingrates in that regard. But none of the Republican orators could have suspected just *how much* gratitude the French revolutionaries expected from Americans, or on what grounds.

IN HIS SECOND DISPATCH TO France written from Philadelphia on May 18, 1793, Genêt tells of his reception by President Washington, who received him "coldly," which was exactly Washington's intention. But Minister Genêt is not discouraged because he knows that "the real Americans" are on the side of the French Revolution.

Les vrais Américains . . . This is not just an idiosyncratic phrase of Genêt's own. It is a critically important element within the French revolutionary ideology. In every country, the partisans of the French Revolution are the only "real" whatever it is. Thus the great French revolutionary historian Jules Michelet, in his account of the liberation of Belgium by the French revolutionaries, distinguishes between *les vrais Belges* and *les faux Belges*.

By any conventional statistical computation, the *faux Belges*—that is, the Belgian opponents of the French incursion—were in a majority, but in terms of the French revolutionary ideology, this is an illusion. The *faux Belges*, not being really Belgian at all, cannot properly be entered into the computation. The only Belgians who are really Belgians, in the logic of ideology, were *les vrais Belges*, the friends of the French Revolution. Similarly, Citizen Genêt is secure in the knowledge that he has the support of the American people, since those who do not welcome him are not *les vrais Américains*. (He was later to wonder whether George Washington was *un vrai Américain*.)

A postscript to this dispatch runs:

> Tomorrow, Citizen, I shall have my first ministerial meeting with Mr. Jefferson, Minister for Foreign Affairs. His principles, his experience, his talents, his devotion to the cause which we uphold, all inspire me with the greatest confidence in him and make me hope that we shall reach the glorious goal which the general interest of humanity must make us desirous of attaining.

That was in Dispatch No. 2. Dispatch No. 3, dated May 31, has nothing to say about that interview with Jefferson. We can safely infer that Jefferson did not fully meet Genêt's expectations, even then. No doubt Jefferson mingled a few words of caution with his compliments, and that would not have gone down too well. Also, Jefferson's official demeanor toward the first envoy of the French Republic may have been less warm than Jefferson personally would have wished. In March, before Genêt's arrival at Charleston, there had been discussions as to how to receive him. Washington had told Jefferson that "Mr. Genêt should unquestionably be received, but he thought not with too much warmth or cordiality, so only as [to] be satisfactory to him."

Jefferson must have been taken aback by this. It did not tally with his understanding, after his December conversation with the president, that Washington had become a convert to the cause of the French Revolution. So Jefferson was already aware that relations with Genêt were going to require delicate handling. This awareness may have been apparent in the Genêt-Jefferson interview.

No official chill in Philadelphia can damp the ardor of the revolutionary proconsul as he takes America by storm: "All America [*L'Amérique toute entière*] has risen up [*s'est levee*] to recognize in me the Minister of the French Republic: the voice of the People continues to neutralize President Washington's declaration of neutrality. I live here amid perpetual feasts."[3]

Dispatch No. 3 ends on a practical note: "The privateer [*corsaire*] *Le Sans Culotte* which I armed at Charleston has captured eight large English vessels."

Le Sans Culotte was operating out of American waters, as were other vessels armed by the minister plenipotentiary and by the French consuls who cooperated
enthusiastically with his revolutionary program. Genêt
obviously assumed that the American administration,
cowed by the demonstrations of "the people's" will,
would not dare to interfere with the development of his
program. Most writers on the subject attribute this
mistaken assumption to the personal vanity of Edmond-
Charles Genêt. Genêt's vanity was indeed a somewhat
enlarged organ, but his mistaken assumption was one
that he shared with the other French agents—mostly
consular—in the United States at this time. It was an assumption drawn not from any merely personal source,
but from a collective experience and a collective ideology: those of the French Revolution. To all French revolutionaries it was axiomatic that the executive must bow
before the popular will, as manifest in popular assem-
blies and demonstrations. French revolutionaries, contemplating the American scene in 1793, had a subliminal
tendency to assimilate George Washington to Louis XVI.
This was not conducive to a realistic assessment of American affairs.

In Dispatch No. 4—June 19, 1793—Genêt for the first time takes Washington personally to task and announces his intention to appeal to Congress against him:

> Everything has succeeded even beyond my hopes: the real Republicans [*les vrais Républicains*] are triumphant, but old Washington [*le vieux Washington*], who differs greatly from the man whose name has gone down in history, does not forgive me my successes, and the enthusiasm with which the whole Town [of Philadelphia] thronged to my house, while a handful of English merchants were thanking him for his proclamation [of neutrality]. He is putting every kind of obstacle in my way, and obliges me to work secretly for the convening of Congress, in which the majority, under the leadership of the finest minds [*les premières têtes*] of the American union will be decidedly in our favor.

Les premières têtes . . . This is clearly a reference to Jefferson and Madison, whom Genêt still believes to be on his side, at this point in his mission.

As WE HAVE SEEN, the proclamation of neutrality occurred before Genêt had presented his credentials. The early debate over Genêt's mission centered on whether tolerance of certain activities of his in the long interval between his arrival in the United States and the presentation of his credentials was compatible with American neutrality.

As Harry Ammon puts it: "In the spring of 1793, basic policy towards France was shaped more by the Secretary of the Treasury, whose influence over the President seemed unshakeable, than by the Secretary of State." Hamilton, as well as Jefferson, had informed Washington of the French declaration of war against England, and it was Hamilton who, a few days afterward, asked his confidant, Chief Justice John Jay, to draft a proclamation of neutrality. The proclamation, in its final form, was based on Jay's draft, and the questions put by Washington to the Cabinet concerning the question of neutrality were drawn up by Hamilton, as Jefferson noted.

For Jefferson, the climate in the Cabinet room, while neutrality was being discussed in April 1793, must have been stiflingly Hamiltonian, laden with heresy.

Jefferson did not advocate entry into war, against monarchist England, on the side of the French Republic, although the mystical "Adam and Eve" side of him must surely have been attracted to the concept of a Franco-American alliance in the cause of Liberty. But Jefferson knew that was out of the question: Washington would not have it, and if Washington would not have it, the country would not have it either. The members of the Cabinet were agreed (for different reasons) that America should stay out of the war that had just begun in Europe. Jefferson accepted neutrality, in practice. But he sought to avoid a *proclamation* of neutrality. Granted the popularity of France, and the unpopularity of Britain, among the American public, a proclamation of neutrality would appear as a snub to France and a victory for Britain. And American Republicans might begin to wonder what exactly Thomas Jefferson was doing in an administration that behaved in that way. As Jefferson put it in a letter to Madison near the end of April, "I fear that a fair neutrality will prove a disagreeable pill to our friends, tho' necessary to keep us out of the calamities of a war."

In these rather trying circumstances, Jefferson, like the pragmatist he usually showed himself to be, when difficult political decisions had to be made, fought a skillful rearguard action. Finding he could not avert a proclamation of neutrality in substance, he managed to keep the word *neutrality* omitted from the proclamation. He also managed to eliminate from the final text some strictures on French revolutionary proceedings that had figured in Jay's draft. More substantially, Jefferson sketched a fall-back position. He questioned the constitutionality of such a proclamation. Was it not an invasion of Congress's power to declare (or not to declare) war? Jefferson did not convince any of his Cabinet colleagues

on that point, but he did convince James Madison. The
Republicans therefore found a way of dissociating themselves from the proclamation—by holding it to be *ultra
vires*—without challenging neutrality in practice. As
Alexander deConde puts it:

> If the administration was not favourably disposed to-
> ward republican France, popular sentiment was. This
> sentiment would, perhaps, spread to Congress and help
> to mold foreign policy. In the newly elected Congress,
> Republicans would, for the first time, have a dominant
> voice; they would control the House, and the Senate
> would be divided about evenly with Federalists. By sup-
> porting a call for a special session and emphasizing the
> role of Congress in the formulating of foreign policy, Jef-
> ferson would hasten the day when his party would have
> an important voice in the conduct of foreign policy and
> could perhaps counterbalance Federalist predominance
> in the Executive Branch.

It can be seen that there was much in common between the direction of Jefferson's thinking and that of
Genêt in April to June of 1793. Both were contemplating
an appeal to Congress against an executive decision—the
proclamation of neutrality. Genêt's ideas on that subject
were far more dramatic, and less well informed, than

those of Jefferson. Still there was a shared general direction of the thinking of these two partisans of the French Revolution, in this early phase of Citizen Genêt's mission. And we have always to keep in mind that the *National Gazette*, known to be under Jefferson's patronage, staunchly supported Citizen Genêt throughout his mission. But what Citizen Genêt failed to see was that the things the *National Gazette* was saying had a specific and limited function. That function was a domestic and propagandist one: to mobilize and develop support for the Republican Party, and in this process to encourage and draw upon the popularity of the French Revolution, this popularity being a major asset of the Republicans in their struggle against the Hamiltonian Federalists. So the *National Gazette* was not a reliable guide to the mind of the secretary of state when delicate policy positions had to be taken. But Genêt could never understand American politics. To that devout French revolutionary, the very existence of forms of American politics affected by domestic issues was a betrayal of the Cause of Liberty, synonymous with the French Revolution.

THE SHEER BRIO OF Genêt's dealings with the British had at first some charms for Jefferson, as we have seen. But by late June, with Genêt still busy arming privateers in American waters, recruiting American citizens, and

disregarding governmental warnings, Jefferson realized
that Genêt was becoming a dangerous liability to the Republican cause, and that leading Republicans would have
to be alerted accordingly. In a letter to James Monroe, on
June 28, 1793, Jefferson wrote:

> I do not augur well of the mode of conduct of the new
> French minister; I fear he will enlarge the circle of those
> disaffected to his country. I am doing everything in my
> power to moderate the impetuosity of his movements,
> and to destroy the dangerous opinion which has been ex-
> cited in him, that the people of the U.S. will disavow the
> acts of their government, and that he has an appeal from
> the Executive to Congress, & from both to the people.

Of course, the "dangerous opinion" in question
was one that the Republican press and the associated
Democratic-Republican Societies were busy propagating
throughout that summer. Jefferson, Madison, and Monroe were at that very time preparing "an appeal from the
Executive to Congress" over the proclamation of neutrality. But all that was *American* politics. It was a different
matter for the representative of a foreign power to join in.
Jefferson is prescient here. Genêt at this time is at the
height of his popularity with Republicans, but Jefferson
sees that this popularity can boomerang against the

Republicans, if Genêt's activity comes to be seen as foreign interference. Of course, from Genêt's point of view, it wasn't foreign interference at all. Genêt was not a mere representative of any old foreign government. He represented *the French Revolution*, which was the cause of all humanity. Genêt was confident that all *les vrais Américains* would view his conduct in that light. Unfortunately—as with the Belgian experience—*les vrais Américains* were outnumbered by *les faux Américains*, though that was not how it looked in the early summer of 1793.

In writing to Monroe, Jefferson was careful in his language: he knew it would not be easy to cure Monroe of his illusions about Genêt. Writing (about a week later) to Madison, who is completely under Jefferson's spell at this time, Jefferson is more outspoken. He writes:

Never in my opinion was so calamitous an appointment made, as that of the present minister of F. here. Hotheaded, all imagination, no judgment, passionate, disrespectful and even indecent towards the P. in his written as well as his verbal communications, talking of appeals from him to Congress, from them to the people, urging the most unreasonable and groundless propositions, and in the most dictatorial style etc. etc. etc. If ever it should be necessary to lay his communications before Congress or the public, they will excite universal indignation. He

renders my position immensely difficult. He does me
justice personally, and, giving him time to vent himself
and then cool, I am on a footing to advise him freely, and
he respects it. But he breaks out again on the very first
occasion, so as to shew that he is incapable of correcting
himself.

Jefferson's complaints are fully justified. But it wasn't
just Genêt. Genêt is acting on both the letter and in the
spirit of his instructions from the Executive Council.
Genêt and the French consular corps in the United
States—*bons patriotes* all—are fervent devotees of a common ideology. Through them, what was working in the
United States that feverish summer was the French Revolution itself, making itself at home on American soil and
in American territorial waters.

Jefferson could have seen that if he wanted to, but he
didn't, or if he did, he never let on. It was politically ex-
pedient to put *all* the blame on Genêt, personally, so that
is what Jefferson did.

In July of 1793, most Americans were unaware that
relations between their government and the minister
plenipotentiary of the French Republic were under severe
stress. The Democratic-Republican Societies, which had
begun to swarm—with the active encouragement of Jefferson and Madison—even before Genêt's arrival, took

Genêt rapturously to their bosom. The Fourth of July in 1793 was an occasion for many Republican manifestations, emphasizing the continuity and affinity of the American and French revolutions, and celebrating French and American friendship. Federalists also had to have their Fourth of July celebrations, of course, but these were 100 percent American things in that year as in others. For the modern reader considering reports of Fourth of July celebrations, the distinction may not always be clear, if only because one emblem had been common to both revolutions and could be used, in retrospect, to symbolize both or either; these two cases being as different as chalk from cheese. "Both" celebrations were Republican, in 1793. "Either" (meaning American-only) celebrations were Federalist. The emblem that could be common to the two types of celebration was the cap of liberty.

When I first read the report of how George Washington had joined in a celebration of the Fourth of July in 1793, I fancied for a moment that even Washington had succumbed to the Francophile frenzy of that summer. The report ran, "and in the town of Alexandria the President of the United States drank with his Virginia neighbours the toast 'Prosperity to the French Revolution,' while the cap of liberty was placed above the American flag and a standard below bore a zestful effusion in praise of liberty."

The toast is anodyne enough. What startles is that cap of liberty—until you remember that the cap in question had been an American emblem before it became a French one. But of course Washington's *Republican* Virginian neighbors—probably about half of the total— would see the cap of liberty as a symbol of the continuity of the two great revolutions, and could hope that Washington saw it in the same light. Actually, he didn't. That celebration in Alexandria was helpful to the Federalists, not the Republicans, for it adopted an address of confidence in Washington "as the virtuous leader of the Republic."

Hardly any of Washington's Virginia neighbors could object to that, of course, but it carried with it an implied rebuke to the Republican press, then sniping at Washington's administration, while supportive of Genêt.

The Cabinet was divided over what to do about Genêt. Hamilton wanted the president to announce publicly his intention of requesting Genêt's recall. Washington was reluctant to go so far, no doubt for fear of the consequences of provoking Jefferson's resignation over transactions connected with the French Revolution. Jefferson's resignation, in such a context, would have had explosive repercussions throughout America in the summer of 1793. Neither Jefferson nor any other member of the Cabinet wanted that. In order to gain time, the Cabinet, on Jefferson's recommendation, decided to put a number of questions to the Supreme Court, leaving the matter of recall in suspense until they were answered.

Genêt was shaken, but by no means chastened, by the repercussions of his defiance of the government. In a dispatch dated July 31, 1793, Genêt writes:

> Mr. Jefferson is the only one I can regard as being on my side [*le seul dont j'aye à me louer*]. He is the object of the hatred of the President and of his Colleagues, although he has had the weakness to sign opinions which he condemns [sic], "privately." In any case, before long we shall be avenged: the representatives of the people are about to assemble and it is from them that will come the thunderbolts which will lay our Enemies low [*qui terrasseront nos Ennemis*] and will positively electrify all America . . . My real political campaign will open with the Congressional session, and it is then that you will judge your Agent.

One can imagine Jefferson shuddering if he had been able to read these lines. It would be impossible to think of a more disastrous congressional lobbyist than Citizen Genêt. The only safe way of maintaining American enthusiasm for the French Revolution was to keep the

French Revolution at a distance, seen through a warm haze. Any whiff of the real thing was fatal. Genêt's high-handed modus operandi kept providing such whiffs.

By early August Washington was clearly very angry indeed, not only with Genêt, but with the Republican press, and implicitly with Jefferson. In notes under the date August 2, Jefferson gives an account of a Cabinet meeting. The relevant part of the account runs:

> Knox in a foolish incoherent sort of a speech intro-
> duced the Pasquinade lately printed, called the funeral
> of George W-n [Washington] and James W-n [Wilson];
> King and judge &c. where the President was placed on a
> guillotine. The President was much inflamed, got into
> one of those passions when he cannot command himself,
> ran on much on the personal abuse which had been be-
> stowed on him, defied any man on earth to produce one
> single act of his since he had been in the government
> which was not done on the purest motives, that he had
> never repented but once having slipped the moment of
> resigning his office, & that was every moment since, that
> *by god* he had rather be in his grave than in his present
> situation. That he had rather be on his farm than to be
> made *emperor of the world* and yet that they were charg-
> ing him with wanting to be a king. That that *rascal Fre-
> neau* sent him 3 of his papers every day, as if he thought

he would become the distributor of his papers, that he could see in this nothing but an impudent design to insult him. He ended in this high tone. There was a pause.

That must have been an awkward pause. Everyone around that table knew the close working relationship between Jefferson and Philip Freneau, editor of the *National Gazette*. When Washington called Freneau a rascal, he was coming perilously close to calling *Jefferson* a rascal.

In the following week tempers were allowed to cool when the Cabinet members reached agreement in the matter of Genêt's recall (after the Supreme Court had refused to give an opinion on the matter). Shortly before August 12, 1793, Washington approved Jefferson's recommendation that the request for Genêt's recall be made in a moderately worded letter to the American minister in Paris. This meant of course that Washington had decided to get Genêt recalled, and that he had also decided to let Jefferson handle the matter in such a way as to do as little damage as possible to American relations with the French Republic.

On August 18, Jefferson sent to Madison a copy of the draft of the message requesting Genêt's recall. In his covering letter Jefferson said, "The addresses in support of the proclmm. [of neutrality] are becoming universal, and as universal a rising of support of the President against Genêt." Jefferson added: "You are free to shew the enclosed to Colo. Monroe."

The implied message from the leader of the Republican Party to his chief lieutenants is clear: Genêt is now more of an embarrassment to the Republican Party than he is to the administration. Leading Republicans are to prepare the minds of party members for news of the request for the recall, and to preempt any tendency to agitate in favor of Genêt.

Meanwhile French ships in American ports were doing their best to introduce the French Revolution to America. At Boston in August the French ship *Concorde* exhibited a banner "proscribing" eleven prominent American citizens as "aristocrats" and enemies of France. Even for American Republican sympathizers, the French Revolution was coming much too close to America in the late summer of 1793.

On August 25, Jefferson reinforced the message to Madison with a more explicit one to Monroe:

> You will perceive by the enclosed papers that Genêt has thrown down the gauntlet to the President by the publication of his letter & my answer, and is himself forcing that appeal to the public, & risking that disgust, which I had so much wished should have been avoided. The in-

dications from different parts of the continent are already sufficient to shew that the mass of republican interest has no hesitation to disapprove of this inter-meddling by a foreigner, & the more readily as his object was evidently, contrary to his professions, to force us into the war. I am not certain whether some of the more furious republicans may not schismatize with him.

Monroe would not care to be associated with "the more furious republicans," though he was a little nearer to them than either Jefferson or Madison was.

"Schismatize": the religious type of invective hitherto applied solely to Federalists (and Burke) is here turned on Republican extremists. Jeffersonian orthodoxy is shifting its center, under the pressure of the excessive proximity of the French Revolution.

The "gauntlet" that Genêt had thrown down consisted of a letter Genêt had addressed to the president and caused to be published after a report that Genêt had threatened an appeal to the president. According to Genêt's dispatch of August 15 to his citizen minister:

Up to now, the *Fayettiste* Washington has annulled all my efforts by his system of neutrality . . . The friends and adherents [of England] in the Council, alarmed by the extreme popularity which I am enjoying, dare spreading a rumor that I wish to stir up the Americans to revolt against their Government, and this weak Government, always afraid of the English, would deserve such an appeal . . . But as the thing [*le fait*] is false, I have just written to General Washington a very strong letter declaring that I ask him to render homage to the truth by declaring that I have never threatened him with anything of the kind [*d'une pareille demande*]. I am waiting his response, which I shall make public, and soon afterwards I shall also publish my correspondence with M. Jefferson, a man endowed with good qualities, but weak enough to sign things which he does not think and to defend officially threats [sic, against Genêt] which he condemns in his conversations and anonymous writings.

On this letter Harry Ammon aptly comments:

All this must have baffled French officials, for the tone of previous dispatches and all his talk about the ultimate effect of public opinion gave the impression that he did plan some kind of appeal. After all was not the promised publication of his correspondence a plea for popular support? Genet seemed to be denying what in fact he was actually doing—seeking popular backing to override Washington's policies.

According to the peculiar terminology of the French Revolution, Washington and Jefferson were—as long as they behaved themselves—*patriotes* belonging to *républiques sœurs*. Both were terms of art. *Patriotes*, in French revolutionary usage, is a much more precise term than *patriots* in English. A *patriote* in any country is a person who puts the interests of the French Revolution first, absolutely and in all circumstances. It's *not* a question of putting the interests of France ahead of one's own country (as a Federalist might see it). The reality is that no country has any legitimate interests of its own distinct from those of the French Revolution. It is the French Revolution that defines the legitimate interests of all countries, and lays down the lines on which those interests are to be pursued. A *patriote*, in any country, was a person who understood and accepted this relationship.

Similarly, a *république sœur* was a country that unreservedly submitted to the French Revolution, *la sœur aînée, la grande nation.* In Europe all the *républiques sœurs* were deemed to have been liberated by the French revolutionary armies and were governed by local *patriotes* who had established their credentials as such to the satisfaction of French revolutionary officers. The most prized characteristic of a local *patriote* was gratitude to the French for having liberated him. This gratitude was expected to be expressed with deferential fervor. Thus when a French revolutionary army liberated a small town in Belgium, the Belgian *patriotes*, of course, came out to welcome them. All then sang the "Marseillaise," but the French soldiers sang it standing up while the local *patriotes* sang it on their knees, in homage to their liberators. That was the kind of thing that was expected of a *patriote* in a *république sœur*.

In the perspective of French revolutionary ideology and terminology, the United States presented a distressing anomaly. From the noises you heard in the streets, you might think this was a *république sœur*, brimming over with enthusiastic *patriotes*. But when you stayed around for a while, you found this was not so at all. The people who had the greatest reputation as *patriotes*—Washington and Jefferson—were deficient in the most basic characteristic of a *patriote*—unquestioning submission to the will of the French Revolution. They did not even seem to understand that submission was what the French Revolution required of them. Thus, in the affair of *La Petite Démocrate*, Washington and Jefferson saw Genêt as defying the authority of the United States. But Genêt, with equal sincerity, saw Washington and Jefferson as defying the only legitimate authority that existed and applied universally: that of the French Revolution. No *république sœur* could have any authority that could avail against that of the French Revolution. The thing was preposterous.

Again, this was not just Edmond-Charles Genêt speaking. It was the French Revolution speaking through Genêt and also through his colleagues, the consular agents. Historian Meade Minnigerode gives examples of revolutionary consular utterances:

Gentlemen who, like the [French] Consul at New York in the midst of the controversies over shipping, spoke of Jefferson as "this Minister of a day and of a Republic that owes us the light of day," who "dares to speak to men representing the most powerful nation on earth in the language of the old tyrants," and instructed the Secretary of State in person to address his complaints and "threats" henceforth to the French Minister. Or, like the Consul at Philadelphia, announced to the world that "no authority on earth has either the right or the power to interpose between the French nation and her enemies"; that "she alone is arbitress and judge of the offensive actions which . . . she is forced to commit against the despotic governments [confederated] to plunge her again into [that] slavery from which she alone has been able to free herself, although abandoned by her friends"; and that police seizure of French prizes by the courts of Pennsylvania in accordance with the President's orders was a procedure "hitherto unheard of," inaugurating what could only be a diplomatic discussion "by an arbitrary act of violence and by military execution.

Thomas Jefferson had admired the French Revolution from afar before 1793, and he would continue to admire it from afar after 1793, though more circumspectly and more tepidly than before. But when the French Revolution actually visited the United States in 1793, in the persons of those Girondin envoys led by Citizen Genêt, Jefferson neither understood nor admired it, and the French Revolution neither understood nor admired *him*.

By the late summer of 1793, Genêt personally was no longer a factor to be reckoned with for Jefferson, but there remained the question of how to cope with the legacy of Genêt. Basically, this was a matter of the management of the French Revolution as an issue in American politics. The Republicans needed to keep American enthusiasm for the French Revolution alive—as one of their major assets in their political war with the Federalists—but they also needed to keep it within bounds and leave the unfortunate Genêt interlude behind them.

From late July on, the Hamiltonians—profiting from the repercussions of the *Petite Démocrate* episode—had been on the offensive and carrying out their own version of "an appeal to the people" with considerable élan, through public meetings and anti-Genêt resolutions accompanied by a press campaign. On August 17, the Hamiltonians carried the war to the capital of Virginia. A meeting in Richmond on that date strongly endorsed Washington's proclamation of neutrality and condemned "all attempts of foreign diplomats to communicate with the people except through the Executive." Madison and Monroe set out to counter the Hamiltonian offensive with belligerently anti-Federalist resolutions. Jefferson quickly called them to order. To get Genêt forgotten, the Republican resolutions needed to be *basically similar* to those of the Hamiltonians, and different only in emphasis. Madison and Monroe complied. The Republican resolutions, like the Hamiltonian ones, would be warmly supportive of the president and include a statement affirming "the principle that foreign diplomats must conduct their negotiations with the executive" and refrain from "appeals to the people." With those points safely embodied, the writers of the resolutions could afford to be expressive of gratitude to France for past help and of appreciation of the French alliance (of 1778 to 1783).

Jefferson's deft handling of "the war of the resolutions" is evidence of the control he could exercise over his own party, in a time of difficulty and danger, and of his skill in damage limitation. As a political general, he had to withdraw his army in good order from an untenable patch of territory. Hamilton had won that battle, but Jefferson would win the political war, seven years later.

On October 11, 1793—a week before the execution of the queen of France—the French Committee of Public Safety agreed to the American request for the recall of Genêt. The news of Genêt's recall by the French authorities reached Philadelphia in mid-January 1794. For Jefferson and the Republicans this was a most happy outcome to the affair. For Jefferson it meant that the *French Revolution itself* had approved his request for the recall of Genêt, so that not even the most "furious" Republican could now claim that that request represented any kind of desertion of the French Revolution. For Republicans in general, the recall of Genêt meant that the French Revolution itself had repudiated Genêt and that American friends of the French Revolution were still faithful to it when they broke off relations with Genêt. The American Republicans needed to keep American enthusiasm for the French Revolution alive—as one of their major assets in the contact with the Federalists—but they also needed to keep it well within American bounds and leave the unfortunate Genêt interlude safely behind them.

Those who were unstinting in their efforts to find excuses for the French government said that the dismissal of Genêt was proof that he had indeed exceeded his instructions. Those who argued in that sense ignored the fact that the government that had recalled Genêt was different from the one that had given him his instructions. So different, indeed, that the one that recalled him had already guillotined all those who had given him his instructions. But American admirers of the French Revolution were not (generally speaking) curious about such transient and sordid details.

Genêt, although recalled at Washington's request, remained in America, under Washington's protection. The new Jacobin government demanded his arrest and deportation, but *le vieux Washington*, that miserable *Fayettiste*, refused because he knew that if Genêt returned to France he would meet with the same fate as those who had given him the instructions he had followed all too faithfully.

So Citizen Genêt, alone of the Girondin elite, survived the triumph of the Jacobins. He married his Cornelia and lived peacefully in America for the rest of his days, without ever returning to France. There is no record indicating that he ever expressed any gratitude to the man whom he had defied and maligned, and who in return had saved his life. But then, according to Genêt's ideas, it was *Washington* who had been ungrateful—to France, which had liberated him, along with all the other

ungrateful Americans. France was wonderful, when con-
templated from America. Genêt and Jefferson could still
agree on that much.

ON FEBRUARY 22, 1794—Washington's sixty-second
birthday—Genêt's mission was formally terminated.
On the following day, the new minister for the French
Republic, Joseph Fauchet, presented his credentials.
Fauchet was well received, his instructions from Robespierre's Committee of Public Safety being most satisfactory to Washington's administration. On behalf of the
committee, Fauchet disavowed "the criminal conduct of
Genêt and his accomplices," forbade all Frenchmen from
violating American neutrality, and dismissed all the consuls who had earlier taken part in arming privateers. Support for the western operations started by Genêt (and
abetted by Jefferson) was also withdrawn. The only unacceptable part of Fauchet's instructions was the request
for the arrest and deportation of Genêt himself—refused
by Washington on humanitarian grounds—and Fauchet
did not press this point.

The conciliatory attitude of the Committee of Public
Safety toward the United States might seem at variance
with the Terror then raging in France, on the orders of
the same committee, but in fact the conciliation of America and the Terror are cognate phenomena. Both reflect

the same reality: the fact that revolutionary France was under siege. A year later, Fauchet's successor, the Thermidorian envoy Pierre-Auguste Adet, succinctly recalled the situation of revolutionary France as it had been at the time of Fauchet's arrival:

> It was in February that [Fauchet] arrived in America; France torn by terrorism, La Vendee in the paroxysm of its devastation, Toulon in the power of the English, the Austrians pushing their light troops into the Department of the Aisne, and already masters of Le Quesnoi, Valenciennes and Conde—such was the situation of the French Republic, as it then appeared in the American public press.

In that forbidding situation, the great Committee of Public Safety, under the guidance of Robespierre and Saint-Just, pursued external and internal policies designed to reduce the number and the power of its enemies. France was not actually at war. The most important of these countries was the United States, now valued mainly as a source of grain for the besieged French Republic. The internal policy was the Terror.

Federalists had their own reasons for not "overreacting" (as we would now say) to the reported excesses of the Jacobins. Federalists had disliked and feared American enthusiasm for the French Revolution since early 1791, when Alexander Hamilton first realized how Jefferson and his friends were exploiting that enthusiasm as a weapon against the Federalists. That enthusiasm had reached a climax early in 1793, with the news of the war between Britain and France, and the arrival of Citizen Genêt. After that, the fall of the Girondins, and their destruction at the hands of the Jacobins, provided a respite for the Americans and for Washington's government in particular. It is true that the Jacobins were doing unspeakable things in France—and Federalists had no doubt of the truth of the reports—but they were scrupulously correct in their diplomatic dealings with America. Washington's government was content to settle for that. Protests against revolutionary excesses would have brought a satisfactory phase in Franco-American relations to an abrupt end, would have been unpopular with most Americans, and would have benefited the American Republicans. (Further, it is unlikely that they would have checked or mitigated the Terror.) No prudent government would have embarked on a course fraught with such adverse consequences, both domestic and international. Washington's government was an eminently prudent one. Franco-American relations remained entirely satisfactory during the entire period of the Terror, from the time its existence became known in

America to its end (January 1794 to July 1794). It was only *after* the fall of Robespierre that Franco-American relations again deteriorated.

Moreau de Saint-Méry, an astute observer resident in America throughout this period, believed that Robespierre had actually been *popular* with Americans generally because the American economy benefited from the wave of emigration caused by the Jacobin Terror.

As for Americans of all classes and all conditions, they expressed sincere sorrow for Robespierre and were filled with consternation at his loss. This was their reason why:

Robespierre made France uninhabitable for all the French. Every man, every gold piece, escaped at the earliest moment, and both took refuge with us, who are in need of men, money and industry. Consider, therefore, how the death of such a one will harm us!

I heard this view uttered a hundred times with a frankness which never made it any easier to tolerate.

However that may be, it is clear that the revulsion of Americans from the excesses of the French Revolution, so often assumed as a fact, did not actually manifest itself, to any significant extent, during the period in which these excesses were at their height.

III

IN THE SUMMER OF 1794 two controversies began that aroused strong feelings throughout the United States and that were associated in the public mind—on both sides—with strongly conflicting feelings about the French Revolution. The first concerned the nomination of John Jay as minister plenipotentiary to the Court of St. James. The second, only apparently unconnected, was the Whiskey Rebellion in western Pennsylvania.

John Jay was a noted Federalist and enemy of the French Revolution. Washington, though deeply suspicious of the French Revolution from the first time he heard of it, had never publicly identified with that position and indeed often spoke of the French Revolution with warm approval, which was, in the early (and apparently moderate-dominated) stages of the revolution, common to most Americans, though especially strong among Washington's opponents. In the spring of 1794 Washington had decided to send a special envoy to London with authority to conclude, if possible, a treaty removing all controversies between Great Britain and the United States. The Republican press and the Democratic-Republican Societies immediately opened an all-out attack on Washington's administration. Once Jefferson had ceased to be a member of that administration, at the end of 1793, the Republicans no longer needed to pull any punches where Washington personally was concerned. Washington's mid–twentieth-century biographers write:

> Armed with the broad authority of his instructions, with Washington's best wishes, and with a private letter from Hamilton meant to amplify the conciliatory spirit behind the mission, Jay left New York [the point of departure for his transatlantic mission]. A thousand cheering citizens [reflecting the views of New York's business community] escorted him to his ship on May 12 but by this time Republican criticism of the appointment was savage. Anti-administration newspapers challenged its constitutionality and prophesied a disgraceful outcome of the venture and in the West effigies of Jay were pilloried and burned. The defensive tactics of the Federalist Press served only to draw new venom from Republican pus. Nor was the President to be spared personally.

Assaults upon his character from the press and from the
rostrums of Democratic societies were the most severe
Washington yet had known.[4]

Washington always smarted, even disproportion-
ately, under this kind of attack, but the attacks did not
cause him to lose his nerve. In this case his counterattack
was brilliant.

Almost simultaneously with the appointment of Jay
to London Washington appointed James Monroe as minister plenipotentiary to the French Republic. It was true
that he was sending to London a person who was known to
be well disposed to Britain. But what was wrong with
that? Was Washington not sending to Paris a man who
was known to be at least equally well disposed to revolutionary France? And this was indeed the case. Monroe
was the most fervent of the prominent Republicans in his
commitment to the French Revolution. He was a *vrai
Américain*, as opposed to Jay, who belonged to the *faux*
variety, from a French revolutionary point of view. (See
pages 91–95 for an analysis of the highly idiosyncratic
French perspective on American affairs.)

Of course, Washington's argument about evenhanded-
ness was no more than a debating point, though quite a
plausible one. Jay was being sent to London to conclude,
if possible, a new treaty of major importance. Monroe's

nomination to Paris was (at least on the surface) a routine diplomatic appointment. But besides its immediate utility in debate, the Monroe appointment had several other political merits. Its primary function, within the Federalist grand design, was to keep the French as happy as might be possible while Washington's government was getting on with what would soon reveal itself as the Jay Treaty with Great Britain.

Also, the Monroe appointment was making an awkward point for the Republicans. If the Washington administration is really as awful as the Republican press say it is, why is one of the most senior and respected leaders of the Republican Party taking office under it? Again, as relations with France are bound to turn sour if the Jay mission succeeds, it will be a Republican, not a Federalist, who will have to take the diplomatic responsibility for the failure of a negotiation with the French Republic.

Finally, as Washington's mid–twentieth-century biographers note, Washington "could take comfort in the knowledge that one of his most consistent critics would be in Paris, not Philadelphia," when news of the treaty broke.

BEFORE THE DEFINITE NEWS of the Jay Treaty reached the United States, it was the Whiskey Rebellion in western Pennsylvania that was at the center of public controversy

in the United States. Formally there was no relation between the Whiskey Rebellion, a tax protest, and the Jay
Treaty. In reality the two themes were related.

The links between the French Revolution and the
Whiskey Rebellion in western Pennsylvania consisted of
the Democratic-Republican Societies and the Republican press: these continued to be enthusiastic for the
French Revolution. At a meeting of 226 elected delegates
from the entire region at Parkinson's Ferry on August 14,
1794, the acknowledged leaders of the Whiskey Rebellion, David Bradford and James Marshall, announced
their adherence to the French Revolution and intention
to imitate it. "There was fiery talk; their would-be Robespierre, Bradford, warned of setting up guillotines (none
of them yet knew that Robespierre himself had just been
guillotined) and declared: 'We will defeat the first army
that comes over the mountains and take their arms and
baggage.'"[5]

But very shortly after that it was already all over. On
November 18 Washington was able to report to Congress
on the bloodless suppression of the rebellion. His reference to the societies was economical, and deadly. The excise law, he said, had been received with "reason and
patriotism" by most Americans, but in four counties of
Pennsylvania there appeared "symptoms of riot and vio-

lence" as "certain self-created societies assumed the tone of condemnation [of the excise]."[6]

On December 25 John Adams—who would succeed Washington as president of the United States—brought the Senate in a body to Washington's house and read aloud the statement adopted by the Senate the day before. The Senate, said Adams, approved unequivocally the use of militia by the president and, moreover, shared his condemnation of the proceedings of "certain self-created societies."[7] An earlier address of the House of Representatives, voted on in November, was quite a groveling declaration, but stopped just short of condemning "the self-created societies."

Washington's reply to the House's pronouncement was masterful and even witty: "It is far better," said Washington, "that the artful approaches to such a situation of things [i.e., actual rebellion] should be checked by the vigilant and duly admonished patriotism of our fellow-citizens than that the evil should increase until it becomes necessary to crush it by strength of their arms."[8] It would be hard to conceive of a more firm and graceful implicit rebuke to the House of Representatives for its failure to endorse the Senate's condemnation of the "self-created societies." The delightful phrase *duly admonished patriotism* accurately describes the condition of the

Republican majority in the House at this time. We know that the House's address would not have been as "strong" (in support of the president) had it not been for Washington's "admonition" and the urgent need to keep the House from endorsing the same.

Jefferson himself was fuming for a while and even rebuked Madison for subservience to the president. In a letter to Madison at the end of December 1794, Jefferson remarks to Washington's reference to "self-created societies" as "an attack on the freedom of discussion, the freedom of writing, printing and publishing." He attributes the attack to the "monarchist" tendencies of Washington's administration: "Their sight must have been perfectly dazzled by the glittering of crowns and coronets." Jefferson does not spare Madison himself, his own most faithful friend:

> And with respect to the transactions against the excise-law, it appears to me that you are all swept away in the torrent of governmental opinions, or that we do not know what these transactions have been. We know of none which according to the definitions of the law have been any thing more than riotous . . . The excise law is an infernal one [which may become] the instrument of dismembering the Union, and setting us all afloat to chuse which part of it we will adhere to.

Jefferson, at this point, is writing as if he has convinced himself that the repression of the rebellion—which was accomplished by November—had in reality been a total failure and that the secession of western Pennsylvania is imminent: "their detestation of the excise law is universal, and has now associated to it a detestation of the government, and that separation which perhaps was a very distant and problematical event, is now near and certain and determined in the mind of every man."[9]

These are, in my opinion, wild and whirling words, as indeed Jefferson himself was later to acknowledge, though only implicitly. This letter falls into the category of "ostensible" letters, that is, letters designed to be shown to people—in this case unconstitutional Virginians, regarding Washington himself as a traitor. It is notable that all of Jefferson's wildest letters—including the one about being willing to see "half the country desolated" rather than let the French Revolution perish—were "ostensible" letters, meant to be shown to Virginians.

As regards relations between Americans and the French Revolution, by far the most important aspect of the Whiskey Rebellion controversy was Washington's condemnation of the "self-created societies." The Democratic-Republican Societies throughout 1793 and

1794 had been the most vociferous apologists for the
French Revolution. Now Washington had clearly implied that these societies had been behaving in a manner
that was unpatriotic and dangerous for the United States.
As the most obvious common characteristic of these societies had been enthusiasm for the French Revolution,
Washington, without even mentioning the French Revolution, was giving an impression that enthusiasm for the
French Revolution was in itself suspect.

And this is something new. Up to November 1794
American Republicans had been able—whenever they
saw fit—to claim that Washington shared their enthusiasm for the French Revolution. The view that Washington approved of the French Revolution seemed to be
confirmed—and was intended to seem so—by Washington's nomination of the violently Gallophile James Monroe as minister plenipotentiary to France.

By the mid-1790s Washington no longer feels a need
to conciliate the Republican opposition in Congress.
Quite the contrary indeed. There is a remarkable coincidence here. Washington's "self-created societies" speech
was delivered on the same day—November 19, 1794—
as the Jay Treaty was signed in London. Washington
could not have known of the precise coincidence, but he
did know that the treaty was about to be signed, that the
struggle over its ratification would be a bitter one, and

that the Democratic-Republican Societies would be the main popular foci of opposition to it in the United States.

In the circumstances, the "self-created societies" speech can be seen as a preemptive strike, discrediting the societies as unpatriotic *in advance* of their expected offensive against the Jay Treaty. They had laid themselves open to such a preemptive strike through the flagrant involvement of local Democratic-Republican Societies in western Pennsylvania—with some backing from other Democratic-Republican Societies—in the Whiskey Rebellion. Washington's thrust against the societies is—ostensibly at least—part of a message that contains no reference to France or Great Britain—the most popular foci of agitation by the societies. The message, as formally delivered, is entirely concerned with a rebellion against the United States and the unpatriotic posture of the societies in relation to that rebellion.

There is no doubt that Washington did regard the conduct of the societies as unpatriotic, and not merely in relation to the Whiskey Rebellion. But he would not have been likely to go public against them in the context of the Jay Treaty had he not judged it necessary to do so in the national interest. He believed the Jay Treaty and stable peace with Great Britain were supremely in the national interest of the United States in 1794–1795. That was one major reason for driving home the message against the "self-created societies."

To stigmatize American manifestations of enthusiasm for the French Revolution was an implicit side effect of that comment—but an entirely acceptable one, from Washington's point of view. After all, the French revolutionaries and their friends in America, in attacking the Jay Treaty, would be drawing on the well-established enthusiasm for revolutionary France in America for all they were worth.

The Democratic-Republican Societies were terror-stricken by Washington's repeated adverse references to them. The years of 1795 and 1796 saw a marked decline in their membership—and consequently in manifestations of enthusiasm for the French Revolution—as compared with 1793 and 1794. Washington's prestige among Americans was still enormous—and remained so throughout the remainder of his life—and his disapproval proportionately chilling. If Washington indicated there was something seriously wrong with the Democratic-Republican Societies, most ordinary people would take his word for that.

The American Republicans had been seriously troubled by the Genêt affair, although they never publicly admitted this. But the decline in *popular* enthusiasm for the French Revolution does not date from Genêt's recall, as some have claimed. That enthusiasm continued up to near the end of 1794. It is only under the chill breath of Washington's "self-created societies" references, beginning in November 1794, that American enthusiasm for the French Revolution begins to flicker and to fade.

THE VERDICT ON WASHINGTON'S demolition of the Democratic-Republican Societies given by James Thomas Flexner, Washington's biographer, seems to me quite an eccentric one.

> Even if for the moment he seemed to have triumphed, even if the adverse effects were slow to come to light, Washington had not behaved with his old surefootedness. All the more because he did not bring forward the general reasoning behind his condemnation of the Societies, he had, for the first time in his career, allowed himself to seem (what he desperately did not want to be) the head of a party. He had stepped down to engage in polemics against one segment of the nation. He should have realized that, however carefully he limited his attack, some rabid individuals would expand it, and that the expansion would be attributed to him.
>
> Washington was not one to confess mistakes or take back anything he had said. Yet he gave the most convincing proof of his realization that he had set out on the wrong

road. As President of the United States, he never again engaged in any public denunciation of any aspect of the opposition. Nor did he ever again make any public statement which could be rationally interpreted as limiting in any way the basic freedoms of the people.[10]

Confident assertions on the basis of no more than a documentary silence are usually the mark of an overconfident assumption, and that is so in this instance. But in this instance there is something odder than that, for Flexner is writing in the teeth of actual evidence, contradicting his claim in the very chapter that ends with the formulation of the claim.

Flexner writes:

As far back as 1786, in objecting to a "Patriotic Society," organized to instruct the delegates from Tidewater Virginia, Washington had stated (although *this* society agreed with his own politics) many of his basic objections to the Democratic Societies. "To me it appears much wiser and more politic to choose able and honest representatives and leave them in all national questions to determine from the evidence of reason and the facts which shall be adduced, when internal and external evidence is given to them in a collective state. What certainty is there that societies in a corner or remote part of a state can possess a knowledge which is necessary for them to decide? What figure then must a delegate make who comes [to the capital] with his hands tied and his judgement forestalled? His very instructors perhaps (if they had nothing sinister in view), were they present at all the information and arguments which would come forward might be the first to change sentiments?"[11]

All this, though formulated almost ten years before the outbreak of the Whiskey Rebellion in western Pennsylvania, was thoroughly and profoundly consistent with Washington's actual course in dealing with all rebellions.

And Washington's handling of the Whiskey Rebellion, once it had taken control of a significant part of western Pennsylvania, was thoroughly consistent with his own and much earlier cautious formulation. As Flexner acknowledges:

Washington also accepted a safety valve to be used in moments of crisis. In denouncing the Democratic Societies, he added to the adjective "self-created" the adjective *"permanent,"* which he usually underlined. He approved of the voters meeting regularly (as in town meetings) to deal with problems which affected only their own localities and the understanding of which was within their experience, but he felt that similar meetings should, on

the level of national policy, be convened only when the
voters saw an emergency. The result of this deliberation
would be incorporation in an address to the President.
Washington felt it his duty to respond to every such address he received with an individual, carefully considered
reply. The process was this direct personal communica-
tion between the neighbourhood and the President.[12]

It is a measure of Flexner's integrity as a historian that
he himself furnishes us with abundant material for understanding both the power and the restraint of Washington's
manner of dealing with the Democratic-Republican Societies and the brilliant success with which he achieved the
utter collapse of the societies in the wake of his—and
Hamilton's—bloodless victory over the rebellions. It seems
perverse then, on Flexner's part, to infer that Washington
regretted a policy that had been successful, whose success
he fully recognized and for which—as Flexner acknowledges—Washington never expressed any regret whatever.
Flexner stubbornly insists that Washington must have *felt*
regret that he had "set out on a wrong road." No politician
in the real world ever experienced regret for a policy that
proved brilliantly successful. The fact that Washington
never publicly gloated over an achievement that now lay
behind him should not be taken as implying that he regretted it.

IV

WASHINGTON'S DESTRUCTION of the Democratic-
Republican Societies, with a few economical words, prepared the way for his successful fights for the endorsement
of the Jay Treaty, first by a majority in the Senate, and
later—most unexpectedly to Republicans—by a narrow
but sufficient victory in the House of Representatives. In
retrospect, the suppression of the Whiskey Rebellion, and
humiliation of its political supporters among and around
the Democratic-Republican Societies, can be seen as the
dispersion and disarming of the most likely force, at
the popular level, of resistance to the Jay Treaty. This was
a well-prepared preemptive strike, as Washington's Republican critics were later ruefully to recognize.

Following Washington's "self-created societies" reference in November 1794, American popular enthusiasm for the French Revolution began to falter, though it
was far from disappearing as yet. Faltering though it was,

that enthusiasm still looked formidable enough in the early part of 1795, and it was vigorously fanned by the French revolutionaries who now appeared to dominate Continental Europe. The Thermidorian politicians in the Directory were intoxicated by what they could still regard as *their* victory—though it was really achieved by French generals, one of whom, Napoleon Bonaparte, was soon to dismiss the Directory, replacing it with his own personal rule. The personal rule was then soon to be formalized by replacing the First Republic with the Napoleonic Empire. Of all that, the first signs were already recognizable in early 1795, though few in America could detect these signs. Washington, who had long before, like Burke, foreseen the transmutation of the First French Republic into a military dictatorship, was one of the very few Americans who understood what was really going on in France and in the French-controlled areas of Continental Europe.

By January 1795 the French were aware of the existence and general nature, though not yet of the precise content, of the Jay Treaty. The Thermidorians, intoxicated by French victories—which they foolishly imagined to be their own achievement—regarded the Jay Treaty as a piece of impudence on the part of a third-rate power toward the new masters of Europe. From Paris, Gouverneur Morris warned Hamilton secretly that the

French meant to cancel the French-American treaties of 1778 and to exclude America from trade with Continental Europe.

On June 15, 1795, Pierre-Auguste Adet, the new ambassador of what was still (just) the French Republic, presented his credentials to President Washington. Adet reported to the Directory the president's reception of him:

> Protestations of friendship to France; wishes for her success; some praise for the President; such was the text of the President's address and of my replies. I would have been touched by the apparent sincerity of his protestations if I had not already been instructed by public opinion, by men who are sincerely attached to our country, that France is the plaything of the master of the Cabinet of Philadelphia.

By "men who are sincerely attached to our country," Adet clearly meant Jefferson, who was in close and constant touch with him at this time and regularly briefing him about Washington.

But could Jefferson really have been supplying an enemy of the United States with ammunition to be used against the president of the United States? It certainly looks like that, and Jefferson clearly meant it to look like that to Adet, but I don't think it was really quite like that.

Jefferson, in my opinion, was playing a double game, something that often attracted him. He was briefing Adet against Washington, but at the same time he was warning Adet not to go too far, and always to keep in mind Washington's great, if undeserved, popularity among ordinary Americans. He wanted Adet to convey to Washington that, if he went ahead with the Jay Treaty, as it now stood, there was a real danger that the French Directory would declare war on the United States. Jefferson must have hoped that, after that warning, Washington would have tried to secure amendments to the draft treaty that would be unacceptable, and there the negotiations would collapse.

This was a miscalculation on Jefferson's part, but not a wild one. Washington's immediate reaction, on first sight of the draft treaty, appeared to be a negative one. From the sequel it would appear that the negative note was a feint: Washington's apparent period of hesitation about accepting the treaty was a deception, or, rather, a *coup de reste*, as in chess, intended to induce both friends and enemies of the treaty to make their positions known. Then the president would know how to proceed.

Washington's primary concern was with the Senate. He would have been aware, both by his own soundings and those of Hamilton, that approval by a majority of the Senate was probable but not certain. As his *coup de reste*,

Washington simply submitted the Jay Treaty for the Senate's consideration, without making any recommendation one way or another.

On June 24, 1795, after a long and brilliantly conducted press campaign by Hamilton in favor of the treaty and eighteen days of stormy debate, the Senate gave its advice and consent to the treaty by exactly the necessary two-thirds majority, twenty votes in favor to ten against. The timing of the announcement of the acceptance of the treaty was left to the president. Before adjourning, the Senate had advised that although the nature of the previous decision might be revealed, the text of the treaty should not be published until the president had decided whether or not to ratify.

Before taking a final decision Washington consulted Hamilton, on whom he had long relied for confidential advice, on timing and presentation. On substance, in relation to foreign affairs (though not finance), Washington generally knew his own mind. In a letter written in his own hand on July 3, 1795, almost four months after the treaty had arrived, headed "private and perfectly confidential," the president stated that he now felt free to communicate with his former Cabinet officer, since the treaty had "made its public entry into the gazette."

Washington went out of his way to make clear that he was not turning to Hamilton as the ultimate expert or with the intention of necessarily doing what Hamilton might advise: he said that he believed Hamilton had given as much attention to commercial matters "as most men" and that his government experience had "afforded [him] more opportunities of deriving knowledge therein" than most American officials possessed. Washington wished "to have the favourable and unfavourable sides of each article stated and compared together," in order to see "the tendency and bearing of them and, ultimately, on which side the balance is to be found."

On receiving Washington's letter, Hamilton wrote Washington a long letter—he later added to it with two supplementary mailings—which ran to forty-one printed pages. He stated that most of the treaty seemed

upon the whole as reasonable as could be expected; the controversial points between the two countries opened the prospect of repossessing our western ports; and offered the United States an escape from being implicated in the European war. The continuation of peace with Great Britain was much more important to American commerce than any merely commercial advantages or disadvantages. The compensation of American pre-Revolutionary debts to Britain that Jay had agreed to would cost less than one military campaign. The terms are not in any way inconsistent with national honour and

all the immediate disadvantages were capable of revision
in a few years.

Hamilton's conclusion was solidly in favor of approv-
ing the Jay Treaty: "The calculation is therefore a simple
and plain one."

Washington thanked Hamilton warmly for his advice, but did not immediately rally to it. Clearly he still
had doubts as to whether the American public at large
was yet ready to embrace a treaty with Great Britain and
break with revolutionary France, which would inevitably
follow the conclusion of such a treaty. To Hamilton,
Washington commented lucidly:

> The string which is most played on, because it strikes
> with the most force the popular ear, is the violation, as
> they term it, of our engagements with France; or, in
> other words the predilection shown in that instrument
> [the Jay Treaty] to Great Britain at the expense of the
> French nation.

How exactly Washington had hit the nail on the head
as regards pro-French reactions is revealed by Jefferson's
report to Monroe, which jubilantly stated that the Jay
Treaty "has, in my opinion completely demolished the
monarchical party here." Jefferson explained that "those

who understand the particular articles of it condemn those articles. Those who do not understand them minutely, condemn [the treaty] as wearing a hostile face to France. The last is the most numerous class, comprehending the whole body of the people."[13]

"The whole body of the people" it was not, as Jefferson well knew, but it was still most of the people, as Washington knew. As citizens of the United States adopted more and more angry pro-French resolutions that might encourage active French intervention, Washington wrote: "I have never since I have been in the administration of the government, seen a crisis which, in my judgement, has been so pregnant of interesting events nor one from which more is to be apprehended."[14]

Washington writes with a remarkably clear perception of the line actually taken by the American Republican leaders, as known to us by Jefferson's correspondence with Monroe.

ANTI–JAY TREATY RIOTS, ON A LARGE SCALE, followed throughout July in Boston, New York, and Philadelphia. They were accompanied by a scurrilous press campaign directed personally against Washington.

The press campaign against Washington in the summer of 1795 was conducted principally by Benjamin Franklin Bache, whose *Philadelphia General Advertiser* and *Aurora* had replaced Freneau's *National Gazette* (defunct since 1793) as the principal organ of the Republican Party. The general direction of the attack is summarized by James D. Tagg, who has made a study of this campaign:

> The attacks were as varied as they were virulent. Included in the catalog of Washington's alleged shortcomings, failures and crimes were: his cold, aloof, arrogant manner; his lack of intelligence and wisdom; and his love of luxury and display. According to his critics, he was both incompetent and unrepublican. He had been a poor general and a lukewarm patriot; he was ungrateful to France; he had conspired to destroy American liberty through a new alliance with Great Britain. . . .
>
> *Aurora* editorials attacking Washington ranged from small two-line attacks to the massive serialized assault by the "Calm Observer" (John Beckley), who successfully showed in 1795 that Washington had overdrawn his Presidential salary.[15]

The involvement of John Beckley in the campaign to defame Washington is particularly interesting. Beckley was a close confidant and confidential agent of Thomas Jefferson, used by him in an earlier campaign to discredit Alexander Hamilton. Beckley's commitment to a "massive serialized assault" on Washington in 1795 strongly

suggests that Jefferson at this time did not merely con-
done the campaign against Washington but was orches-
trating it from behind the scenes, in the 1795 phase of
Jefferson's "retirement."

WASHINGTON'S SEVENTH ANNUAL address was to be delivered in the Senate chamber on December 8, 1795.
Those who were there to hear him expected him to be
on the defensive and probably alarmist about a perceived
threat to the nation. These expectations were not ful-
filled. On the contrary.

Washington's address opened with the following words:

> Fellow citizens of the Senate and House of Representa-
> tives: I trust I do not deceive myself while I indulge the
> persuasion that at present the situation of our public af-
> fairs has afforded just cause for mutual congratulation
> and for inviting you to join me in profound gratitude to
> the Author of all good for the numerous and extraordi-
> nary blessings we enjoy.

He then enumerated various blessings: satisfactory
relations with various Indian tribes and with the emperor
of Morocco; prospects of peace with Algiers and Madrid.
As Flexner puts it: "So far so good, but what about
Jay's Treaty? Ah, Washington was getting to it now."

Washington stated that, as everyone knew, the treaty had been approved by the Senate

upon a condition which excepts part of one article. Agreeably thereto and to the best judgement I was able to form of the public interest, after full and mature deliberation, I have added my sanction. The result on the part of his Britannic majesty is unknown. When received, the subject will, without delay, be placed before Congress. Prudence and moderation on every side could now extinguish all the cases of external discord which have menaced our tranquillity.

As Flexner accurately notes: "The pro-French legislators who were continually crying that the Jay Treaty was anti-French could hardly believe that Washington would move on from foreign affairs without mentioning France. But even in their incredulity, they may have recognized that the President had outflanked them, the discussion had been of nations 'which have menaced our tranquillity.' This omission of France could be taken as recognition of common interest."

Washington's handling of foreign affairs, which he had thoroughly mastered, was always well informed and often subtle, as it was on this occasion. He had left the French as yet with no leverage against him.

The opposition to Washington at home was also weakening, as Washington sensed. He had now the Senate firmly on his side, and with the readily available support of private subscriptions he could have bypassed the House. But he decided not to do so, but to bring the House to heel. Circumstances had become propitious for this endeavor. Flexner writes:

> As a matter of fact the opposition had been weakening even during the months when [it seemed that] no-one would join Washington's cabinet and he seemed most exposed. Jefferson moaned that, although the Federalists had been 'in a defile where they might be finished', they were escaping. He attributed this partly to the prestige of the President, partly to the detailed defence Hamilton had published of every clause of the Treaty; partly to the violence of the opposition which had so alarmed the merchants that they no longer dared oppose the treaty lest the government be torn apart.

The government of what was still the French Directory had thought up an ingenious, if somewhat fatuous, scheme for embarrassing—they hoped—the man whom they still called General [rather than President] Washington. On New Year's Day, 1796, French minister Pierre-Auguste Adet delivered to Washington a present from the French government to the American legislature. "It was a tricolour made of the richest silk and highly ornamental with allegorical paintings in the centre, a cock standing on a thunderbolt, at two corners, bombshells bursting. The edges were hirsute with fringes and tassels of gold. The flag was accompanied by two addresses which spoke in the most ecstatic terms of brotherhood between France and the United States."[16]

Washington agreed to transmit the address to Congress, without comment. He also announced the nomination of the leading pro-French member of Congress as minister plenipotentiary to France. This, again, was a carefully calculated move.

ON FEBRUARY 29, 1796, Washington, having received only the approval of the Senate and without waiting for the reaction of the House of Representatives, declared the Jay Treaty the law of the land. He must have known that the House would react adversely, and they duly did.

On March 2, 1796, Edward Livingston, a leading man among the anti-Federalists in the House of Representatives, presented a motion requesting that the president submit to the House "every relevant document in the executive archives—Jay's instructions, all relevant correspondence, etc.—which might throw light on the treaty and on how it had been negotiated."

During two and a half weeks of debate the House agreed with Madison that Washington might hold back documents that existing negotiations might render it improper to disclose. But the House voted down another amendment, also proposed by Madison, that Washington might, in general, use his judgment on what might, in the public interest, be reserved. Thus the bill that was passed by the House on March 24, 1796, by a vote of 62 to 37, claimed for the House not only the right to reconsider treaties that had constitutionally become the law of the land, but the right to unrestricted supervision of the acts of the executive.

Washington received the document with the laconic statement "that he would take the request of the House into consideration."[17]

Madison, who had done so much to shape the Constitution of the United States, understood that document far better than any other member of Congress and knew also how thoroughly Washington understood it. And Madison must have shuddered at the coming confrontation and its implications for the future.

Washington delivered his answer to the House on March 30, 1796. The answer stated that the House had no constitutional right to executive documents except in the case of "an impeachment which the resolution has not expressed." The need for caution and secrecy in foreign negotiations had made the Constitution entrust them to the legislative body that had "a small number of members" (that is, the Senate, not the House). That treaties were obligatory if ratified by the president with the Senate's approval was understood by foreign nations and had never before been questioned by the House. The state conventions that had ratified the Constitution had, as various of their proceedings showed, understood that the treaty-making provision included commercial treaties. Following its spirit of amity and mutual concession, the Constitution had created a balance by giving special powers to the Senate as a protection to the small states.

Most deadly of all to his opponents, Washington reminded the House that the journals of the Constitutional Convention had been entrusted to him personally for safekeeping. The journals showed that a proposition that no treaty should be binding until ratified by law had been specifically *rejected*. It being perfectly clear that the assent of the House was not necessary, and it being essential that the boundaries fixed between the different branches by the Constitution should be preserved, Washington's duty forbade his compliance with the House's request.[18]

The Republican leadership—Madison excepted—had somehow convinced themselves that Washington would not "hazard a break with the House." They had expected that if he did not agree, he would suggest a compromise. His flat refusal struck like a bombshell. Fisher Ames, a leading Federalist, wrote that the majority party in the House seemed "wild on its being read."

Flexner, often critical about Washington, has no doubts at all about this one. Flexner writes:

> It was now clear that the leaders of the House's effort had made a colossal tactical error. Although securing the executive papers would have increased the prestige of the House and probably have given them an advantage in attacking the treaty, the documents were by no means necessary to the House's basic contention. The appropriations could be denied by refusing rather than passing a bill, which would have given the President no opportunity for a veto. If the President adhered to his so far invariable rule of not moving out of his province to comment on legislative action in which the executive was not involved, his convictions need never have been expressed. But now his prestige had been brought to bear against the claims of the House. How could he so grievously have let the Republican leaders down? Why, oh why, had they stirred the old man up?

V

THE SENATE HAD RATIFIED the Jay Treaty by the necessary two-thirds majority. The House of Representatives had originally rejected it by what looked like a comfortable majority. But under the pressure of a brilliant press campaign by Alexander Hamilton, bringing out the advantages of the treaty for Americans and the weakness of the arguments against it, the House also, by a majority of three votes, ratified the agreement. Washington's political victory, achieved against what had looked like heavy odds, was now complete.

After the Congress had risen, at the end of 1794, the Republican leaders ruefully acknowledged that Washington had completely outmaneuvered them. Madison felt that the Republicans had been defeated by Washington's personal prestige and popularity (thrown decisively against the Republicans at the end of 1794 with the "self-created societies" reference). Jefferson now fully agrees with this interpretation, which he claims to have "always observed." Jefferson wrote to Monroe in June 1795:

> Congress has risen. You will have seen by their proceedings the truth of what I have always observed to you, that one man outweighs them all in influence over the people who have supported his judgement as against their own and that of their representatives. Republicanism must lie on its own oars, resign the result to its pilot and themselves to the course he thinks best for them.[19]

No doubt Jefferson must have confided some qualms on the subject to Madison, during the congressional proceedings, or he could hardly write to him in this retrospective strain, but he certainly gave no public indication of any qualms at the time.

Jefferson subsequently made overtures to Washington, hoping for a reconciliation (which would have helped his own future electoral prospects), but it seems clear that this attempt was coldly rebuffed by Washington. Historian Dumas Malone has left a long and typically sentimental account of this conversation, but one has only to be capable of reading a bit between the lines to see that Washington was not impressed by Jefferson's overture. Washington knew that Jefferson had actuated and still inspired the Republican press that had been attacking Washington obliquely while Jefferson was still Washington's secretary of state and had been harassing Washington openly and recklessly (mainly over the Jay Treaty) since Jefferson's "retirement." In the circumstances, Washington's comment on the "extravagant and indecent language" of the Republican press, like his earlier reference to Jefferson's press creature, Philip Freneau, as "that rascal Freneau," in 1793, is an oblique reference to Jefferson himself, as Jefferson knew.

To say, as Dumas Malone does, that Jefferson "must have been touched" by this evidence of Washington's extreme sensitiveness is a good example of Malone's tendency to sentimentalize politics in general and his hero Jefferson in particular.

In any case there is no known example of any further exchanges of any significance between Washington and Jefferson.

VI

WASHINGTON WAS, OF COURSE, now exposed to fero-
cious attacks from the remaining champions of the
French Republic. Adet, the French minister plenipotentiary in Philadelphia, who had formerly been cooperative
with Washington's government, was now required by his
own government to denounce Washington's government. Having insisted that the Jay Treaty was in effect a
treaty of alliance with England, Adet announced that he
had been recalled. France would send no other representative to the United States until "the executive of the
United States returns to sentiments and measures con-
formable to the interests of the [French] alliance and the
sworn friendship between the two nations."

Adet's action was on the instructions of an enraged
French government and was therefore entirely pre-
dictable. But another and far wilder series of attacks
came—or seemed to come—from a more unexpected

quarter: Tom Paine, still resident in France. Paine was the man whose great tract, *Common Sense*, had years before been so powerful in stimulating George Washington to espouse the independence of the United States. Paine now aimed this barb directly at the president's heart. The title was *Letter to Washington*.

The epistle, which ran to many pages, was in part an enlargement of an abusive letter that Paine had sent to Washington personally in September 1795. This letter (which Washington had not answered, as was his usual negative method of coping with abusive letters) had upbraided the president for not having intervened officially to get Paine out of a French revolutionary prison. According to Paine's letter, Washington's failure to claim Paine as an American citizen was a deliberate act of treachery. Paine asserted that Washington had conspired with Robespierre to have Paine guillotined for fear that Paine would otherwise expose his own monstrous behavior.

In his many pages aimed at demonstrating that "almost the whole of your administration" was deceitful and perfidious, Paine—or whoever drafted the publications he signed—assumed that any action that displeased French public opinion or did not further French interests was pro-British, contrary to treaty obligations, and damaging to the reputation of the United States.

Stating that "it is time that the eyes of America be opened upon you," Paine traced Washington's whole career in a crimson parade of insults. Washington's Fabian tactics during the revolution (which the Paine of *Common Sense* had once praised) showed him a general of majestic incompetence and timidity. The Constitution he had supported (which Paine had once considered "the admiration and wonder of the world") Paine now called "a copy, not quite so base as the original, of the British Government. . . . If you are not great enough to have ambition, you are little enough to have vanity."

Paine's peroration—or the peroration signed by him—read as follows: "As to you, sir, treacherous in private friendship (for so you have been to me, and that in the day of danger) and a hypocrite in public life, the world will be puzzled to decide whether you are an impostate [*sic*] or an impostor, whether you have abandoned good principles or whether you ever had any."

Washington agreed with the British satirist Peter Porcupine that Paine's attack was something more than personal; it was inspired by the French government.

I believe it was more than inspired. I think it was written, at least for the most part, by a hack in the pay of the French government. *Common Sense* was a brilliant pamphlet, excellently written. *Letter to Washington* turns absurd through its excessive and obsessive violence. Jefferson continued to patronize Paine—and he did not re-

pudiate Paine's pamphlet. But he took good care not to
endorse it publicly, for he knew it to be outrageously offensive to the great majority of the American people.

RELATIONS BETWEEN WASHINGTON and the British
government improved dramatically near the end of
Washington's presidency, with the appointment of a new
British plenipotentiary to Washington. After the House
had given in on the Jay Treaty, the congressional session
had proceeded without any more fireworks. The British
had delighted Washington by quietly evacuating the
frontier forts and bases. Washington was personally
gratified at the recall of the ever-complaining and disagreeable British minister plenipotentiary George Hammond (who did not hide his personal dislike and, indeed,
contempt for Washington). Robert Liston, who replaced
Hammond, was described as a "middle-aged and middle-
class Scot who had risen to high responsibilities despite a
lack of family connections." Of Liston's relations with
Washington, Flexner writes: "Liston was as conciliatory
as Hammond was contentious; he did not meddle in
American politics; he shared with Washington a passion
for farming and he had a delightful wife. The Listons became close friends to the Washingtons."[20]

Mrs. Liston's memoirs are probably the most informed and penetrating impressions of Washington that
have been preserved. She wrote:

His education had been confined; he knew no language but his own and he expressed himself in that rather forcefully than elegantly . . . Letter writing seemed in him a peculiar talent. His style was plain, correct and serious. Ill-natured people [i.e., some Democrats] said that Washington did not write his own public letters, answers to addresses, etc. This is not true. I have known him to write in his usual impressive manner when no person was near to aid him; and which may seem conclusive, he has always written better than the gentlemen to whom the merit of his letters was ascribed.

VII

CHAPTER 32 OF THOMAS FLEXNER'S *Anguish and Farewell*
opens with the words "Washington's Farewell Address
ranks in popular acclaim with the Declaration of Independence and Lincoln's Gettysburg Address. Thus the
rumour that it was written not by Washington but by
Hamilton has shocked or delighted generations with a
subversive or debunking way. Fortunately, the evidence
exists to determine exactly what took place."

The evidence does indeed exist, and Flexner sets it
out in masterly fashion in the fifteen pages of his chapter
32, "Washington's Farewell Address." As my readers
must have noted, I have often been critical of Flexner's
comments on Washington, but I can find no flaw in the
penetrating analysis that makes up the body of chapter 32.

As Flexner shows, in the spring of 1796 Washington
went through his files and pulled out the draft of a
farewell address that Hamilton had prepared to his

specifications when he had intended to retire at the end of his first term. He resolved to include that text verbatim to show not only that "such an address was written but that it was *known* also to *one or two of those characters* [Madison and Jefferson] who were now most vigorously attacking his government."

The old address proved that he had not wanted a second term. The corollary, that he had no personal motive for wishing to extend the power of the executive, would serve "to lessen in the public estimate the pretensions of that party to the patriotic zeal and watchfulness on which they endeavour to build their own consequence at the expense of others." And the realization that his wish to retire was nothing new should "blunt if it does not turn aside" accusations that he was now withdrawing because of fallen popularity and despair of being reelected.

Sitting down to write his new address, "Washington specified that Madison had been 'privy to the [previous] draft'"; and then Washington cut out Madison's name and phrase. The draft he now copied out stated that he had done his best and hoped he would be forgiven any involuntary errors.

The drafts then continued with a statement of general principles, but, as these were to be retained in the final draft, and can be considered then, there is no need to set them out at this stage.

Then, as Flexner neatly and properly observes: "Washington wrote in anger one of those paragraphs which affirm what they deny!"

The paragraph ran:

As this address, fellow citizens, will be the last I will ever make to you, and as some of the gazettes of the United States have teemed with all the invective that disappointment, ignorance of facts and malicious falsehoods could invent, to misrepresent my politics and affections— to wound my reputation and feelings—and to weaken, if not entirely destroy, the confidence you have been pleased to repose in me; it might be expected at the parting scene of my public life that I should take some notice [of] such virulent abuse. But, as heretofore, I shall pass them over in utter silence.

After this rather absurd tirade Washington continues in a vein of self-justification for three more long paragraphs. But the *tone* of the paragraphs gets calmer. One can sense that Washington is cooling down, having got his sense of grievance off his chest, as we would put it.

And the proof that he no longer wished to go on record with what he had drafted is that he had not immediately made public his draft, but sent it to Hamilton. Knowing Hamilton as well as he did, Washington must have known that Hamilton would advise him to amend that draft quite radically. Which Hamilton duly did.

At about the end of April 1796, Washington showed his yet incomplete draft to Hamilton. Hamilton prudently said that so important a paper required "serious consideration" and that he would be happy to help Washington revise it. Washington promised to mail the paper, when finished, to Hamilton in New York. On May 10, Hamilton wrote Washington reminding him of his promise.

Flexner writes:

> On the 15th Washington sent what he stated was his only copy; he had not even kept his preliminary notes. If Hamilton thought it best "to throw the whole into a different form" he shall go ahead, but nonetheless return Washington's own draft with amendments. Showing that he himself had misgivings, Washington authorized Hamilton to discard the "egotisms" (however just they may be) if you think them liable to fair criticism . . . notwithstanding some of them relate to facts which are little known to the community.

In that "however just" and that "notwithstanding" one can sense some of the wistfulness of a frustrated author.

Hamilton, however, as Washington must have known he would be, was ruthless in his editing.

On July 30, 1796, Hamilton wrote Washington that he was "sending herewith a certain draft . . . it has been my object to render this act importantly and lastingly useful." He had "eschewed all immediate controversies" to embrace "such reflections and sentiments as will wear well, progress in approbation in time and redound to future reputation."

This was an altogether new text. Hamilton had started on his other task of revising Washington's own text, but the longer he thought about it the less "eligible" it seemed. It was "awkward," seemed to imply that Washington would not be believed unless he presented evidence, and "I think there are some ideas that will not wear well." When he had both speeches before him the president could judge.

Washington's first reaction was one of dismay at the sheer length of Hamilton's draft. But he told Hamilton he would give the draft "the most attentive consideration."

The president duly did so, and the result was perfectly satisfactory for Hamilton. After several serious and attentive readings Washington decided that he preferred Hamilton's main draft to all other versions. It was "more copious on material points, more dignified on the whole and with less egotism."

As Flexner duly notes: "Hamilton's Main Draft became the basis for what is known as Washington's Farewell Address." Flexner also notes, and more profoundly: "The ideas Washington found expressed in Hamilton's Main Draft proved to be, with very few exceptions, his own."

No man was more familiar with Washington's way of thinking than Hamilton was, and he followed it with great assurance. Very occasionally Hamilton deviated slightly from Washington's mode of thought. Hamilton's passage on religion expressed sentiments that Washington had never put on paper. The president accepted, with only verbal changes, the statement that "whatever may be conceded to the influence of reformed education on minds of a particular structure," it was too much to expect that national morality could prevail without "religious principles." However, another of Hamilton's sentiments was more than Washington, as a deist, could accept. He changed "nor ought we to flatter ourselves that morality can be separated from religion" to read "let us with caution indulge the supposition that morality can be maintained without religion."

Flexner's conclusion to his account of Washington's farewell address is in my view impeccable. It runs:

The address could correctly be attributed to Hamilton if it expressed Hamilton's own ideas. This it only did insofar as Hamilton's ideas coincided with Washington's. When he did try to slip in something of his own with which Washington did not agree Washington almost always recognised the thought as not his own and cut it out. Thus the Farewell Address was as much Washington's as any Presidential paper is likely to be that has been drafted by an intimate aide. If all such documents were attributed to the speech writers, American history, particularly that of recent times, would be set out differently and surely less accurately.

That Washington's Farewell Address was conceived in its existing form and largely composed by Hamilton is a fact. Yet it is also a fact that the famous document is correctly styled "Washington's Farewell Address."

With every word of Flexner's conclusion to his analysis of Washington's farewell address I find myself in full agreement.

Notes

PART ONE

1. The funeral oration was delivered at the request of Congress, December 1799.
2. John C. Fitzpatrick, ed., *Writings of George Washington*, vol. 30.
3. Conor Cruise O'Brien, *The Great Melody: A Thematic Biography and Commented Anthology of Edmund Burke*, p. 387.
4. Morris, *Diary of the French Revolution*, vol. 1, pp. 373–374.
5. "Gouverneur Morris," *Dictionary of American Biography*.
6. In Morton and Bertram, eds., *America's Ten Greatest Presidents*.
7. The history and particulars of this incident may be seen in Spark, *Life of Gouverneur Morris*, vol. 1, p. 339.
8. Ron Chernow, *Alexander Hamilton* (New York: Penguin Press, 2004).
9. Quoted in Richard Norton Smith, *Patriarch: George Washington and the New American Nation*, p. 24.
10. Syrett, ed., *Papers of Alexander Hamilton*, vol. 11, pp. 484–485.
11. Boyd, *The Papers of Thomas Jefferson*, vol. 20, p. 27.
12. Ibid., p. 286.
13. Ibid., p. 737.
14. Hamilton (using the initials *TL*) in the *Gazette of the United States*, July 25, 1792.

15. Thomas Jefferson to George Washington, September 9, 1792.
16. Ibid.
17. Frank L. Mott, *Jefferson and the Press* (Baton Rouge: Louisiana State University Press, 1943), pp. 24–26.
18. Boyd, *The Papers of Thomas Jefferson*, vol. 20, p. 29.
19. Cullen, ed., *The Papers of Thomas Jefferson*, vol. 23, pp. 25–27.
20. George Washington to Thomas Jefferson, October 20, 1792.
21. Cullen, ed., *The Papers of Thomas Jefferson*, vol. 23, pp. 21–22.
22. *Pickering Papers II* (171 Massachusetts Historical Society), quoted in Joseph Charles, *The Origins of the American Party System* (New York: Harper and Row, 1956), p. 51.
23. Lyndon Johnson, when asked why he chose to reappoint J. Edgar Hoover as FBI director; quoted in the *New York Times*, October 31, 1971.

PART TWO

1. James Thomas Flexner, *George Washington: Anguish and Farewell, 1793–1799*, p. 17.
2. *National Gazette*, Philadelphia, March 2, 1795.
3. Genêt, Dispatch No. 3, May 31, 1793.
4. Douglas S. Freeman et al., *George Washington's Biography* (New York: Scribner, 1948–1957), vol. 7; John A. Carroll and Mary W. Ashwall, *First in Peace*, p. 154, n. 50.
5. Elkins and McKitrick, *The Age of Federalism*, pp. 475–476.
6. Freeman et al., *George Washington*, vol. 7, p. 221.
7. Ibid.
8. J. M. Smith, ed., *Republic of Letters* (New York: 1995), vol. 2, p. 862.
9. Jefferson to Madison, December 28, 1794; Smith, *Republic of Letters*, vol. 2, pp. 866–867.
10. Flexner, *Anguish and Farewell*, chap. 19, p. 192.
11. Ibid., p. 188.
12. Ibid., p. 189.
13. Freeman et al., *George Washington*, vol. 34, p. 263.

14. Ibid., p. 256.

15. Tagg, *Attack*, p.195; Freeman et al., *George Washington*, vol. 7, p.154.

16. Freeman at al., *George Washington*, vol. 34, p. 10, n. 25.

17. Ibid., vol. 35, pp. 2–5.

18. Conor Cruise O'Brien, *The Long Affair*, chap. 6, p. 234.

19. Flexner, *Anguish and Farewell*, chap. 31, p. 283.

20. Ibid., p. 284.

Index